THE
NEW
MESSENGER

A BOOK OF THE
NEW MESSAGE
FROM GOD

THE
NEW
MESSENGER

AS REVEALED TO

Marshall Vian Summers

THE
NEW
MESSENGER

Edited by Darlene Mitchell
Cover and interior: Designed by Reed Summers

ISBN: 978-1-942293-17-0
NKL POD Version 8.0
Library of Congress Control Number: 2016911945

Publisher's Cataloging-in-Publication
(Provided by Quality Books, Inc.)

Summers, Marshall Vian, author.
  The new Messenger / as revealed to Marshall Vian
Summers.
  pages cm
  "A book of the New Message from God."
  LCCN 2016911945
  ISBN 978-1-942293-17-0
  ISBN 978-1-942293-18-7 (ebook)

  1. Society for the New Message--Doctrines.
  2. Spiritual life--Society for the New Message.
  I. Society for the New Message. II. Title.

BP605.S58S8345 2016   299'.93
                     QBI16-1317

The New Messenger is a book of the New Message from God and is published by New Knowledge Library, the publishing imprint of The Society for the New Message. The Society is a religious non-profit organization dedicated to presenting and teaching a New Message for humanity. The books of New Knowledge Library can be ordered at www.newknowledgelibrary.org, your local bookstore and at many other online retailers.

The New Message is being studied in more than 20 languages in over 90 countries. *The New Messenger* is being translated into the many languages of our world by a dedicated group of volunteer student translators from around the world. These translations will all be available online at www.newmessage.org.

The Society for the New Message
P.O. Box 1724   Boulder, CO 80306-1724
(303) 938-8401 (800) 938-3891
011 303 938 84 01 (International) (303) 938-1214 (fax)
newmessage.org newknowledgelibrary.org
email: society@newmessage.org

We shall speak of God, the Higher Authority.

––––––––––

The Higher Authority is speaking to you now,
speaking through the Angelic Presence,
speaking to a part of you that is the very center
and source of your Being.

––––––––––

The Higher Authority has a Message for the world
and for each person in the world.

––––––––––

The Higher Authority is calling to you, calling to you down
through the Ancient Corridors of your mind,
calling to you beyond your beliefs and your preoccupations.

––––––––––

For God has spoken again and
the Word and the Sound are in the world.

From *God Has Spoken Again*
Chapter 3: The Engagement

THE
NEW
MESSENGER

—————⌒—————

TABLE OF CONTENTS

INTRODUCTION

The New Messenger is a book of Revelation given by the Creator of all life to the human family through the Messenger Marshall Vian Summers.

Here God is revealing the origin, lineage and mission of the Messengers of God who, at different times in human history, have been sent into the world to receive and present New Revelations to the human family. Now at this turning point in the history and evolution of our world, God has sent a New Messenger into the world to receive a Revelation unlike anything that has ever been given before.

Down through history, the Creator has given Revelation and Wisdom to meet the growing needs of people and nations at different times and in different parts of the world. Through the Messengers of the past, God's progressive Revelations have flowed into human awareness, advancing human civilization and re-awakening the experience of the Divine Presence in the world.

God's progressive Revelations now continue anew through a New Message from God, delivered through a New Messenger, a man named Marshall Vian Summers. The Messenger has been engaged in a long and mysterious process of Revelation. This process began for him at the age of 33 and has continued for over three decades. Working through most of these years in obscurity, with only his family and a few assistants with him, he has received the largest and most comprehensive Revelation ever given to the human family.

The New Messenger is but a small part of the larger text of the New Message from God. The words of the New Message are a direct communication from God, translated into human language by the Angelic Presence that watches over this world, and then spoken through the Messenger Marshall Vian Summers. This spoken communication is then recorded, transcribed and is being compiled into a complete text by the Messenger himself. This is the first time in history that the Voice of Revelation has been recorded and is now being made available for people everywhere to hear for themselves.

The Voice of Revelation continues to speak through the Messenger. The Word and the Sound of God's communication are now being heard around the world.

Why does the world need a New Message from God? Why is this happening now? The New Message states that it is here to alert, empower and prepare the human family to meet the critical and escalating needs of our time as we now face Great Waves of environmental, political and economic upheaval and the hidden reality of contact with intelligent life in the universe. To face and navigate challenges of this magnitude, we need a New Message from God. Here the New Message makes clear that the traditions of the past cannot prepare us for the thresholds before us now, especially in a world of increasing religious violence, division and disintegration.

The New Messenger is the third book of Volume 1 of the New Message from God. It contains 13 individual revelations, each given at different times and places during the Messenger's journeys in the world. *The New Messenger* contains many of those revelations from the Source concerning the Messenger himself. Who is he? Why was he chosen? How was the Revelation actually delivered through him? How can you know that he is real and authentic? And how is he connected to the Messengers of the past?

These are questions that all people may ask. Now God has spoken again with a series of revelations that answer these questions and many more. Through the books of the New Message, God is revealing the true identity of God's current and past Messengers: their selection, their preparation, their relationship to one another and the true meaning of their appearance and emergence in the world.

The New Messenger teaches that all the Messengers of God are members of the Angelic Assembly that oversees the world. Across human history, this Assembly, in response to the Plan of God, has sent into the world one of their own at certain times and places to receive an original Revelation from the Creator. These are the Messengers of God. The coming of a New Messenger represents the opening of the next chapter in the progressive Revelation of God's Will and Plan for the world.

The New Message teaches that God's presence and communication are transmitted into the world at many different levels: through the spiritual mind of Knowledge in each person, through teachers who offer instruction and guidance through existing traditions, through reformers who endeavor to correct and renew these traditions and through prophets who can bring original warning and direction concerning imminent change and events in the world. At every moment, God is moving and communicating in the world, through a myriad of expressions and demonstrations of inspiration, forgiveness, compassion and cooperation between people.

Yet *The New Messenger* reveals that it is through Messengers that the Creator speaks to the entire world, presenting a whole new reality of understanding and awareness that is meant to touch the lives of people in all nations, cultures and religions. It is at great turning points that God moves to touch the world all at once, to move the human family in a new direction and to prepare humanity for the immense evolutionary thresholds that will determine its success and survival in the future. The arrival of a New Messenger signals that such a threshold has been reached, and that God is now speaking to the whole world.

Messengers appear in the world very infrequently, many centuries or even millennia apart, and have been greatly misunderstood over time. They have been imagined to be perfect and immaculate individuals, to perform miracles to impress the masses, to be pure reflections of God or even to be a direct appearance of God incarnate. Here the human imagination amplifies itself over time, clouding and distorting the true lives and stories of these rare individuals and the real meaning of their appearance in the world, both in the past and now in the present.

Through the books of the New Message from God, the real origin, identity and journey of Messengers both known and unknown are being clarified and revealed anew. Here we are shown that the Messengers are both human beings and also members of the Angelic Assembly, selected and prepared beyond this world to enter into human form as a Messenger of God and to receive God's New Revelation for the world. While they are in the world, the Messengers are imperfect, fallible and susceptible to the many hazards and influences of human life—and yet they carry a presence that burns within them like a sacred fire. They carry the presence and power of the greater reality of Creation beyond the world, and they seek to extend this to all who can receive God's New Revelation for that time and the times to come.

The New Messenger reveals the mission and calling of Marshall Vian Summers, the living Messenger now in the world. Here we are invited to understand the Messenger for our time, and to receive the gift that he brings. Here we are given a lifeline to the mysterious reality of our Ancient Home beyond the world and to those who sent us into the world with a purpose to fulfill: to live a life of true inspiration, relationship and service to others. This is the gift and demonstration of the Messenger—that each of us may remember and return to our true identity and allow this to express itself through us in our time in the world.

Though it appears to be a book in the hand, *The New Messenger* is something far greater. It is a calling and a communication from God to you. This is a living communication from the Creator of all life to the human family, and the communication is still flowing through the Messenger to this day.

Remarkably, you have found the New Message from God, or it has found you. It is no coincidence that this is the case. This opens the next chapter in the mystery of your life and of your presence in the world at this time. The door opens before you. You need only enter to begin.

As you enter more deeply into the New Message from God, the impact on your life will grow, bringing a greater experience of clarity, inner certainty and true direction to your life. In time, your questions will be answered as you find growing freedom from self-doubt, inner conflict and the restraints of the past. Here the calling and the gift of the Messenger will come alive in your life, reminding you always that there is a greater life you are destined to live.

New Knowledge Library

ABOUT THE NEW MESSAGE
FROM GOD

*T*he New Message from God is a living communication from the Creator of all life to the heart of every man, woman and child on Earth. This communication is here to ignite the spiritual power of humanity, to sound God's calling for unity amongst the world's nations and religions and to prepare humanity for a radically changing world and for its destiny in a larger universe of intelligent life.

The New Message from God is the largest Revelation ever given to humanity, given now to a literate world of global communication and growing global awareness. It is not given for one tribe, one nation or one religion alone, but instead to reach the entire world, a world very different from the ancient world of the former Messengers. Never before has there been a Divine Revelation of this depth and magnitude, given by God to all people of the world in the lifetime of the Messenger.

The New Message from God has not entered the world through the existing religious authorities and institutions of today. It has not come to the leaders of religion or to those who garner fame and recognition.

Instead, God's New Message has entered the world as it has always done. It has come quietly, unlooked for and unannounced, given to a humble man chosen and sent into the world for this one task, to be a Messenger for humanity at this great turning point.

At the center of the New Message from God is the original Voice of Revelation, which has spoken the words of every book of the New Message. Never before has the Voice of Revelation, the Voice that spoke to the Messengers and Prophets of the past, been recorded in its original purity and made available to each person to hear and to experience for themselves. In this way, the Word and the Sound are in the world.

In this remarkable process of spoken Revelation, the Presence of God communicates beyond words to the Angelic Assembly that oversees the world. The Assembly then translates this communication into human language and speaks all as one through their Messenger, whose voice becomes the vehicle for this greater Voice—the Voice of Revelation.

The words of this Voice were recorded in audio form, transcribed and are now made available in the books of the New Message. In this way, the purity of God's original spoken Message is preserved and given to all people in the world.

The Messenger has walked a long and difficult road to bring the New Message from God to you and to the world. The process of Revelation began in 1982 and continues to this day.

At this time, The Messenger is engaged in compiling over three decades of spoken Revelation into a final and complete testament— The One Book of the New Message from God. This new testament will be divided into six volumes and possibly more. Each volume will contain two or more books, and each book will be organized into chapters and verses. Therefore, the New Message from God will be structured in the following way: Volume > Book > Chapter > Verse.

In order to bring this spoken communication into written form, slight textual and grammatical adjustments were made by the Messenger. This was requested of him by the Angelic Assembly to aid the understanding of the reader and to convey the Message according to the grammatical standards of the written English language.

In some instances, the Messenger has inserted a word not originally spoken in the Revelation. When present, you will often find this inserted word in brackets. Consider these bracketed insertions as direct clarifications by the Messenger, placed in the text by him alone in order to ensure that ambiguities in the spoken communication do not cause confusion or incorrect interpretations of the text.

In some cases, the Messenger has removed a word to aid the readability of the text. This was usually done in the case of certain conjunctions, articles, pronouns and prepositions that made the text awkward or grammatically incorrect.

The Messenger alone has made these slight changes and only to convey the original spoken communication with the greatest clarity possible. None of the original meaning or intention of the communication has been altered.

The text of this book has been structured by the Messenger into verse. Each verse roughly signals the beginning or ending of a distinct topic or message point communicated by the Source.

The verse structure of the text allows the reader to access the richness of the content and those subtle messages that may otherwise be missed in longer paragraphs of text that convey multiple topics. In this way, each topic and idea communicated by the Source is given its own standing, allowing it to speak from the page directly to the reader. The Messenger has determined that structuring the text in verse is the most efficacious and faithful way of rendering the original spoken revelations of the New Message.

The rendering of this text is according to the Messenger's original will and intention. Here we are privileged to witness the process of preparation and compilation being undertaken by the Messenger, in his own time, by his own hands. This process stands in stark contrast to the fact that the former great traditions were largely not put into written form by their Messengers, leaving the original messages vulnerable to alteration and corruption over time.

Here the Messenger seals in purity the texts of God's New Message and gives them to you, to the world and to all people in the future. Whether this book is opened today or 500 years from now, God's original communication will speak from these pages with the same intimacy, purity and power as on the day it was spoken.

CHAPTER 1

THE WILL OF HEAVEN

As revealed to
Marshall Vian Summers
on May 17, 2011
in Glenwood Springs, Colorado

Many people in the world are awaiting the return of their Savior, their Maitreya or their Imam. But God has sent a New Message into the world, a Message to prepare humanity for the great change that is coming here and for its encounter with intelligent life in the universe, an encounter that will be far more precarious and dangerous than most people truly recognize.

Human spirituality is eroding away in the world, the true nature of human spirituality. The deeper nature of each person is becoming ever more remote as your societies become increasingly technological and secular. The divisions between religions are so severe and so damaging, even the divisions within religions will add a great deal to human conflict and suffering in the future, as they are now.

To honestly look at the world is to realize that its mounting difficulties are exceeding human capacity and understanding. The Great Waves of change coming to the world exceed what individuals and institutions can fully comprehend and address.

Humanity has come to a great turning point. It cannot return to its former state. It cannot go backwards in history. It cannot simply reaffirm the divided and contentious beliefs of its religious traditions, which were all initiated by God.

God's Revelation must now come again and has come again, and the Messenger has been sent into the world—a humble man, a man without great social position, a man without great personal assertions and accomplishments, a man whose life has been preserved and directed for this purpose alone.

People will argue, of course, unwilling or unable to reconsider their position and to open themselves to the New Revelation. They think they understand God's Will and Purpose for the peoples of this world. They think they understand what Revelation means and when it can occur. They think they understand.

But who can understand this fully? Who has the wisdom and the breadth and the capacity to understand this fully? Surely this must exceed human comprehension. And surely there must be enough humility and honesty for people to realize that they cannot predict when and how the Creator of all the universes will speak to this one tiny little planet.

But human ignorance and arrogance unite into a dangerous combination, a combination that is vehement and oppressive, that is jaded and highly opinionated. It is polarized and will continue to divide the human family—a division that can only weaken you in the face of the great change that is coming to the world.

The New Message comes here in a pure form, and for the first time you will be able to hear the Voice of Revelation. It was a Voice like this that spoke to Moses and Jesus, the Buddha and Muhammad and the other great Teachers who have remained hidden throughout the course of human history.

There is no time for error now. The risks are too great. Everything is being done with the New Revelation to make it very clear. It provides its own commentary and its own teachings, for these cannot be left up to human interpretation only.

The hour is late, and humanity is unprepared to face a new and declining world and to face the realities and the difficulties of emerging into a Greater Community of life in the universe.

You are at a great threshold. For you individually this means that your life is being accelerated to meet this threshold, to prepare for this threshold and to engage with this threshold.

But how can this be done without a New Revelation from God? There is not a person on Earth who has the wisdom, the capacity and the comprehension to deal with everything humanity will be facing as it passes through this threshold into a new and more challenging world.

Who on Earth can prepare humanity for life in the universe, the great engagement—an engagement that is already taking place, in secrecy, carried out by groups who are here to take advantage of your ignorance and superstitions?

If you are truly honest, you must recognize that no one has this breadth of understanding, this capacity. No one in the world understands the Greater Community of life. And what people think are projections of their fears and their fantasies, neither of which is an accurate portrayal of what you will be facing in reality.

The true nature of human spirituality has now been so clouded, so distorted, so overlaid with tradition and ritual and interpretation that even the great traditions of the world, which can provide the steps that you must take, require a unique and highly gifted teacher to navigate everything else that has been added over the decades and centuries.

Religion has become a palliative. It has become a distraction more than an illumination. It has become something that people [use to] run away from the world to seek comfort and consolation instead of a preparation to engage in the world in a greater and more profound way.

The Creator knows all this, of course. It is beyond debate at a higher level. It is beyond speculation. It is beyond ideology. It is beyond the theology of one religion contending against the theology of another religion. That is a human problem created by human misunderstanding and the limits of human capacity and wisdom.

You may argue against the Revelation, but it is the only Revelation, and it will be the only Revelation. Whether it is accepted or denied, this is it.

God is not preoccupied with this one world. But God is aware of this one world—a very small place in a very great universe.

The Angelic Presence that oversees this world is translating the Will of the Creator into words and application, teachings and commentary that the people of the Earth can understand and apply today and tomorrow and the days to follow.

You are asked to receive, not to judge.

You are asked to prepare for the world, not to use religion as a form of escape.

You are asked to honor your deeper nature and to take the Steps to Knowledge so that its reality can become apparent to you.

You are asked to end your ceaseless conflicts and to never think that you can conduct violence here on Earth in the name of God, for that is an abomination. There are no holy warriors. There is nothing holy about war.

You are asked to learn and to prepare for a new world and to prepare for the realities and challenges and opportunities of emerging into a larger arena of intelligent life in the universe.

You cannot teach yourself these things, for you do not know enough. And to argue against it is only to project your own limits and misunderstanding.

The New Message is being brought to the people—not to the experts, not to the leaders, for they are too invested in their position, and, as a result, they either cannot see what is coming, or they are unable to communicate the truth to those who follow them.

The Revelation gives the individual tremendous power, but also tremendous responsibilities. If you are guided by the power of Knowledge within yourself, the deeper intelligence that God has placed within you, then there can be no violence or war and conflict. There is only the effort to create positive and mutually beneficial arrangements with others. And that is the work for the intellect. That is the great challenge before you, a challenge so great it will occupy all of your energy if you are to undertake it successfully.

The Revelation is beyond the realm and the reach of the intellect. It is beyond the realm and the reach of beliefs and ideology. For God does not create belief. God does not create ideology. God only gives you wisdom and clarity and a high standard to live by. You are either able to adopt these things, or you are not.

To adopt them, you must adopt them compassionately, without using them as a weapon to oppress others or to condemn others. To condemn others to Hell and damnation is to misunderstand God's Revelations, both present and in the past.

To claim that there can be no new Revelations is to proclaim your arrogance and ignorance and to think that you know more than the Creator. For no one on Earth knows what God will do next. Even the Angelic Presence does not know what God will do next, so what person can make such a claim? Surely it is the epitome of ignorance and arrogance.

No one on Earth can proclaim that Jesus is the only pathway to God when God has created other pathways. Who are you to say such things? This is misunderstanding and confusion. This is trying to place your beliefs above and beyond others' beliefs, to make your teacher, your representative, the greatest or the only one to be followed. This is not the Will of Heaven. This is the ignorance of humanity.

The world you will be facing will require immense human cooperation, compassion and contribution, or it will be a battleground over who has the remaining resources of the world, [over] who can protect their wealth while other nations fail and collapse.

The demands upon humanity will be so great and it will take a great compassion and wisdom to respond to this. But the peoples are too divided. The religions are too shattered. This group opposes that group in the name of their national sovereignty or the Will of God, and it is all set in motion to collapse into chaos.

That is why there is a New Revelation in the world. Here you do not praise the Messenger as a God. You honor him as the Messenger. Here you do not proclaim your ideas over another, but realize that ideas are only the tools to be used by the greater strength within you and that the true truth, the greater truth, resides beyond the realm of the intellect, which was never designed to comprehend the greater realities of life.

The Will of Heaven is for humanity to unite and to prepare so that it may survive the Great Waves of change and prepare for its engagement with life in the universe in such a way that human freedom and sovereignty in this world may be protected.

You are facing a non-human universe where freedom is rare and where free nations and peoples must exercise great discretion and great care amidst the presence of many more nations where freedom has been suppressed or where it was never known before.

The demands of the Greater Community are tremendous. You cannot be engaged in constant conflict here on Earth and be able to survive and remain free in this larger arena of life. It is a matter not of perspective or belief. It is a matter of necessity.

For nations to survive environmental decline in this world and increasing political and economic upheaval and difficulty, you will have to cooperate with each other. Instead of fighting, you will have to find ways to provide enough food, water and energy for the people of the world. That will be the prevailing and dominating need of the future here on Earth.

People who think otherwise are living in the past. Their assumptions are based upon the past. They cannot see what is occurring in their midst. They cannot ascertain what is coming over the horizon.

They are living in a shell of their own beliefs and assumptions and are blind to the realities of the world today and tomorrow. They think engagement with the universe will be the result of human exploration, but that is rarely ever the case in the universe. Intervention occurs when nations become stronger and more united. That is when the challenge to freedom and sovereignty really begins.

Your education about the universe and your preparation for living and surviving in the new world are so great and tremendous, they have required a New Revelation from God. The clarification of the nature, purpose and unity of the human spirit must now be emphasized beyond all other things, or humanity will not find the strength or the unity to respond to the great change that is upon you.

A New Revelation brings great correction and clarification, which are necessary now if all the religious traditions of the world are to add wisdom to the human family and not merely add to its partisanship, conflict and contention. They each have a contribution to make. They are all important. One is not greater than another. To think like this is not to understand the Will of Heaven, for it is only a united humanity that will be able to contend with the challenges of living in a new world and with the greater challenges of preserving your freedom and sovereignty amidst the presence of greater forces in the universe.

This is the time. You are living at a time of Revelation. It is a precious time. It is a difficult time. It is a confusing time. It is the time of great consequence.

You are amongst the first to respond to the New Revelation. It is for a purpose that this is so. It is no accident that this is so. You who are still trying to plan your own fulfillment in life do not yet realize you have a greater destiny here, a destiny that will be uniquely expressed in your life, but it is a destiny you will share with others, for no one is in the world by accident now.

Everyone was sent here to contend with the conditions of the world. But this preparation occurs at a deeper level of the mind, at the level of Knowledge. This is the part of you that has never been separate from God. It is the part of you that was and is your true identity. It was Knowledge that brought you into the world. It is Knowledge that will carry you through the world. It will be Knowledge that will emerge with you beyond the world.

The separated are redeemed through Knowledge. The wicked are reclaimed through Knowledge. The foolish are made wise through Knowledge. This is how God redeems not only the human family, but all of Creation that is living in Separation, which is represented by the physical universe that you can only imagine.

It is the Will of Heaven that you respond to the New Revelation. It is the Will of Heaven that you take the Steps to Knowledge—patiently; without presumption; setting aside your beliefs, your preferences and your fears as you proceed so that you may engage with a greater strength, a greater integrity and a great purpose within yourself.

It is the Will of Heaven that this awareness and preparation be shared with others and that you become a vehicle for sharing it very simply, by pointing to the New Revelation.

It is the Will of Heaven that humanity will grow up, emerge out of its reckless and contentious adolescence to become the wise stewards of this world, to preserve the lifegiving resources of this world and to become a free race in a universe where freedom is rare and is rarely valued.

It is the Will of Heaven that you end your ceaseless conflicts, for you cannot afford to destroy your peoples and your cities now. You will need all the resources of the world, all the resources that you have, to contend with the Great Waves of change that are coming.

You are not living in the past. The old world has passed. You are living in a new world—a world with an unstable climate and changing environmental conditions, a world of diminishing resources, a world of ever greater fragility, ever greater uncertainty, where even human civilization itself is imperiled.

But who will see this? Who will hear this, not with their ideas or their opinions or their beliefs, but deeply, more profoundly? Who has the courage to face this? Who has the humility to face the New Revelation? Who can admit that God has more to say to humanity and give up self-righteousness and all of the admonitions and declarations that accompany it?

The Will of Heaven and the intentions of humanity are still very far apart. But the times grow dark. The hour is late. And there is no more time for foolishness and denial.

It is the time of Revelation. It is the gift to humanity, to be received or rejected. It is the future of humanity, to be fulfilled or to be destroyed. It is the promise of humanity, to be realized and expressed or to be squandered and wasted. This is a great decision, not only for people elsewhere, but for you, within yourself.

Everything is based on the decisions of the individual, and that is why the New Message from God speaks to this very directly. It does not simply prescribe a new belief system, a new yoke of ideology under which everyone must yield and be oppressed. People will have to work out the details. But the motivation must be true. The awareness must be there.

There must be greater clarity about what you are dealing with and will have to face in the future, and this will moderate your errant and destructive behavior. This will give you pause before you condemn or attack another people or nation. This will moderate extremism and fundamentalism and all of the arrogance and ignorance that manifests itself with such vehemence and eloquence in the world.

You must hear this with your heart. Do not delay, for every day is important now. Time cannot be wasted now.

The Messenger is here. He will not be here forever. You are blessed to hear him and to meet him if possible. He carries within him the Revelation, beyond what is produced in a book or a recording.

Receive him. Hear him. And your life will demonstrate the proof of the truth that abides with him, in him, and through him.

CHAPTER 2

THE ORIGIN OF THE MESSENGER

As revealed to
Marshall Vian Summers
on August 1, 2012
in Boulder, Colorado

People have no idea what it means to be a Messenger or how Messengers are selected or prepared. They want to worship heroes or deny them altogether.

They want to believe the Messenger is the Message, but the Message is always greater than the Messenger. People will base their whole view and approach on their attitude towards the Messenger, but the Message is always more important.

People cannot live with the Message, so they obsess over the Messenger. But they do not understand the Messenger. They have no idea where the Messenger comes from and how the Messenger is selected above and beyond everyone else. Many people think there cannot be one Messenger. There must be many Messengers, or they themselves should be a Messenger.

Into a world of Separation, one representing a greater union will be misconstrued and misperceived. It cannot be avoided.

The Angelic Host, the Angelic Assembly, selects the Messenger for every particular world where a Messenger is required. And a Messenger is only selected at times of great change, difficulty and opportunity for a race, for a given world. Such great turning points only come very infrequently.

Despite the great events that are occurring in your world at any given time, Messengers will only come very infrequently. In the interim, there will be prophets—giving warnings or setting standards for behavior. There will be visionaries. There will be reformers. There will be advocates.

But the Messenger brings a whole new reality. This individual is not simply one who gives warning of the great hazards of the future or the present day, or provides higher standards or a greater vision of peace, cooperation and equanimity amongst the human family, for there are many who can do this. But only a Messenger from God can bring an entire new reality and change over time the awareness and the consciousness of large numbers of people, even affecting the attitudes of the entire human race.

A prophet cannot do this, for prophets speak of what is occurring now or in the near future. Their prophecies are not for all time and all peoples. They are specific to certain peoples and places and events.

Those who teach a higher standard, they must reinforce a standard that has already been given, many times over, by others who were called to such a valuable service.

But the Messenger brings a whole new reality. They are not charged with meeting every need of the day or resolving every problem or crisis of the hour. They are bringing something to change the whole approach and future of humanity.

Messengers are condemned and crucified and destroyed because people do not get what they want from the Messenger. They do not get wealth or greater security or advantages or special favors—endowments from God.

The Messenger points to the present and to the future and brings a new reality into the world. People who are needy and ambitious do not get what they want in the moment from this, and so they turn away from the Messenger. They deny the Messenger. They condemn the Messenger. They are looking for someone who is going to benefit them right now in the ways that they want and prescribe. They have no idea what they are looking at. They have no idea what they are judging. They have no idea what their greater needs really are—the need of their soul.

This is a dilemma for all peoples in the world—rich or poor, from any nation or culture or religious affiliation. They are not yet aware of the great need of the soul. Those few who are, are reaching within their traditions or beyond their traditions. They are reaching to find this connection inside, this connection with God, and this connection with their future and their destiny and their purpose for being in the world. Everyone else is like cattle grazing in the field, only content to have feed for the day and more pleasures for tomorrow and to be protected, either legitimately or illegitimately, from the hazards of the world.

God speaks to those who have and those who have not. God speaks to those who rule and those who are ruled. God speaks to those who are honest and those who are dishonest. God speaks to those who are rich and those who are very poor.

The Messenger brings a Message for them all. He is not a reformer. He is not just an advocate. He is not just a visionary. He is not just a prophet warning of the consequences of hazards in the world today. He brings a reality for everyone who can receive him, in humility and honesty. And his presence in the world will cast in contrast everything else that is deceptive and manipulative and self-serving and grievous and unforgiving and angry.

But the Messenger is not perfect, for none of the great Messengers have been perfect. And the Messenger is not a god, for none of the great Messengers have been gods.

His origin is from beyond the world. He was selected and prepared by the Angelic Presence to enter into the world at a certain place and a certain time.

His destiny was to become basically educated about humanity and the human condition and to be insulated from the world sufficiently that his greater promise and calling could occur later in his life when he reached a point of maturity.

His life was planned out, you see, unlike everyone around him. His life was really planned out and watched over. This is the reality of all the Messengers. And it is the reality of the Messenger who is in the world today, bringing a New Revelation from God.

For God has spoken again to prepare humanity for the hazards of living in a diminishing and declining world and the great and unseen dangers of contact with invasive forces from the universe, who are here to take advantage of human weakness, ambition and disunity.

The Messenger was given the Message beyond the world, not intellectually, but imbued at a deeper level of the mind, beyond the realm and the reach of the intellect. Who can understand this? Who in the world today can understand this, but a very few?

He would be a humble man. He would be educated, but not highly educated. He would be influenced by the world, but not highly influenced by the world. He would be observant of others, but not captivated by others. He would have to remain available, open and receptive through all the formative years of his life.

Very difficult to achieve, this is, without Divine oversight. Held back from great careers. Held back from committing in relationships until he met his true partner. Held back from interests and hobbies. Held back from becoming an advocate or a reformer. Held back for years and years, failing the standards of society, failing the expectations of society, failing the expectations of family—waiting, preparing for the moment of Initiation.

For God's Messenger this time, it happened at the age of 33. He would have to wait a long time. The Message was within him, but beyond his awareness. He was carrying it like a secret cargo. For the cargo must be secret so it cannot be tampered with. It cannot be revealed prematurely. It cannot be misused, misallocated and misunderstood. It must wait for the Initiation, the Great Rays of Initiation, which would strike him so forcibly that it would shatter his life and send him in a new direction entirely.

People think that the great Messengers are all very saintly, very pure, never having made an error in life. This is foolishness. Of course they all made errors in life. Some of them have suffered greatly for it.

What made them Messengers was the power of the Message imbued in them and their ability to withstand the seductions, the tragedies and the pressures of the world to such a time where their Initiation could begin. And this could not have happened without Divine oversight and careful management of their lives. People think this oversight is available to everyone, but that is not the case.

In all cases, the Messengers did not know who they were or what they were carrying or what it would mean for the future until the point of Initiation and the process of Initiation that would ensue that would carry them forward through many thresholds into the future. Time and place were very important here, and the degree of support they received from certain individuals was very important here.

This is truly a unique individual in the world, and always has been. Though their [worldly] origins are ordinary and humble in most cases, they end up being the most important people in the world.

They are sent by the Angelic Presence. They are imbued with the Message, which is greater than them, which is greater than their understanding, which is greater than anything they could conceive of themselves. It has the Power of God within it. It has the power of Initiation.

No Messenger could think this up. No Messenger could conceive of this and construct this. This is not a teaching based upon an eclectic approach or a revised version of existing traditions. Spiritual teachers around the world in all traditions do this, but the Messenger brings something greater.

The Messenger is not magnificent. The Messenger is not so awe inspiring that everyone around him immediately recognizes this person's importance and uniqueness.

This has never been the case for God's Messengers. They were treated very poorly. They were ignored, or denied, or brutally treated—hardly recognized by those around them. Only a very few had this recognition, and they would play an important part in the Messenger's development and early ministry and later successes.

Now for the first time, the power of Revelation is being given around the world all at once—not in one tribe, not in one specific region, not in one important place in the world. For the world now is connected, and the Messenger will speak to the whole world, and the whole world can turn against him as well. The opportunity is immense, but so are the hazards involved.

As always, religious figures will be threatened once his voice becomes heard, once the impact upon people grows, once his Message begins to take hold. And though he is not here to attack governments or overturn brutal dictatorships or to be revolutionary in this way at all; though he brings peace, cooperation and equanimity, he will be treated like an enemy by those who claim to be religious, by those who claim to represent God and God's Will, by the followers of all the previous Messengers.

Many will consider him an enemy and a threat. This shows you how far they really are from the Source of their own traditions and how weak is Knowledge within them, the greater mind that God has given to all people.

It will be easier for the ordinary person to recognize the Messenger. It will be easier for the person who has few preconceived notions and no investment in their position in society to recognize the Messenger.

You can deny him. You can disclaim him. But he has the Message, and he is bringing it forth, in the purest form possible.

You can even hear the Voice of Revelation now, which was never possible before and which has never happened before. Yes, Angelic Voices have been heard speaking to very specific things, and this has been recorded at times, but a New Message from God has never been recorded in its pure form.

To recognize the Messenger, you must have the eyes to see and the ears to hear. You must be willing to set aside your preconceived notions and your grievances against religion and your firm beliefs about God, religion and spirituality to have a pure and real experience.

The Messenger will not condemn religions of the world, but he will provide in contrast the very essence of their Teachings that has been lost, forgotten or denied.

He will bring a new reality into the world that will require all religions to reassess their primary and fundamental ideas and beliefs. Though he has no violence within him, he will turn the tables upside down by his proclamation, by his presence in the world and by the Revelation itself.

People will become obsessed about who he thinks he is or says he is or who he could be because they are afraid of the Revelation. They cannot deal with the Message, so they will become preoccupied with the Messenger. They will complain. They will accuse him of things. They will think that for the Message to be true, the Messenger has to meet their criteria. They will complain, as if they know what the criteria for the Messenger are. Such foolishness and arrogance, but many people hold these views and base their ideas upon them.

Oh, he must give people what they want, or they will not want him. All Messengers have faced this fundamental and unavoidable dilemma.

He is not here to give you what you want. He may not even give you what you think you need in the moment. But he is giving you the pathway to your own personal revelation, to your restoration and your redemption. And he is bringing it to you in the clearest possible terms.

He is speaking to a literate world now, so the Teaching is not clothed and concealed in pastoral terms, or anecdotes or stories that have to require human commentary for people to understand their meaning.

The Revelation is given pure and simple. But it is so deep that people will have to be with it in a new way, for it is not an intellectual enterprise. It is a matter of the heart and of the soul.

The Angelic Assembly understands the predicament of bringing something this powerful and pure into the world, and the crisis it will create for people as to whether they can receive and accept this, and the challenge it will give to them to reform their own lives and to establish their connection with Knowledge, the greater intelligence that God has given them, which waits to be discovered.

It is for this reason that the Revelation has provided the Steps to Knowledge at the very beginning of the Revelation that the pathway would be established and not created later by imaginative peoples, and that the clarity and purpose would be established clearly, and not re-established later by those who did not know the Messenger.

The risk of corruption is so great. The risk of misinterpretation is so great. The risk of misunderstanding is so great. That is why the Revelation is repetitive—repeating over and over again its purpose, its aim, its pathway and the obstacles and problems that people will have to face to begin to gain a true relationship with their deeper nature, and to have the chance of discovering their greater purpose in the world, and all the forgiveness and reconsideration that this will require, given how they view themselves and the world today.

The Messenger does not bring peace. He brings challenge. He brings opportunity. He brings restoration. He brings work. He brings true relationship. He brings the Divine Will and Purpose into the world.

He brings the Revelation that can save humanity from collapse within the world and from the risk of subjugation from beyond the world. He brings things that are so great that people have never even thought of them before.

He speaks to the needs of the future as well as the present. He speaks to the needs of the people a century from now who are facing a world catastrophically changed. He speaks to those who will have to face the Greater Community of life in the future and even those who are experiencing contact at this moment.

He brings the solution to a thousand questions and problems, beyond what people know of today—what will secure and create human freedom and sovereignty in the universe, where freedom is rare, where everything will be done short of invasion to take advantage of a weak and unsuspecting humanity.

People know nothing of this. People know nothing of the real hazards facing the world today. They are living in their own little dream, preoccupied with their needs and problems. They have no idea what is going to threaten human civilization, both from within and from without. But the Revelation brings this awareness.

For only God can reveal what life is like in the universe, and this is part of the Revelation. Only God can reveal what is coming over the horizon for humanity, and this is revealed in the Revelation. Only God can speak to the deeper needs of the heart and the soul, and this is the center of the Revelation. From the needs of the whole world, both now and in the future, to the fundamental and core needs of you the individual, at this moment, the Revelation speaks of all these things, for they are all connected, you see.

The Messenger speaks of living a greater life in service to a world in need. Surely, this need is growing with each passing day and will escalate beyond what people estimate today.

He calls people out of their miserable attempt at self-fulfillment, their tragedies, their predicaments, their entrapment, [calling] people out of political and social and religious oppression to find the voice that God has put within them to find and to follow.

For this, he will be denied and condemned by those who have invested in other things, by those whose views are threatened; whose position in life is questioned; whose values, ethics and firm beliefs are thrown into doubt by his proclamation and by the nature of the Revelation itself.

The Angelic Presence knows that if he can reach enough people within the span of his time, the Revelation will take hold in the world. But many things have delayed the Messenger. People have not responded who were destined to do so. There have been financial setbacks, grave serious illness and the great challenge of penetrating the ignorance and preoccupations of humanity.

That is why anyone who can respond to the Messenger must truly respond. And time is of the essence, for he is an older man, and his presence in the world is of critical importance for the future of humanity.

This time, the Angelic Presence presented the Message first before the Messenger would even proclaim himself. In that way, the Message has been preserved. It has been printed. It has been established. Even if the Messenger should meet calamity tomorrow, the Message is here, and there are enough people now to speak for it and carry it forward. This is to prevent usurpation and corruption, for the Message speaks clearly, without a great need for human commentary or intervention.

Yet the Messenger contains more than what is in print and what has been recorded. That is why if you can reach the Messenger and hear the Messenger, you will hear things beyond what has been printed and recorded.

For he carries the Message within him like a fire. It burns. But it warms the soul and illuminates the landscape. The Fire of Knowledge within the Messenger is unlike any fire in the world. It is so powerful even he can barely stand it for long periods of time.

Your relationship with him is important. You do not yet realize its importance. But he must be seen correctly. He must be seen from the soul and the heart. He must be heard, and the nature of Revelation must be understood sufficiently so that you can understand the great opportunity this is giving to you and to the world.

For it will be centuries before another Messenger is sent. This is it. This is the one. This is the real Message for the world for this time and the times to come.

Fail to respond here, and the consequences will be great for your life and for the world. You will not find your destiny. You will not find your calling. You will be lost at sea with everyone else—groping, searching, suffering. Knowledge within you will be alive, but you may never find a way to connect with it. And your grievance against the world will grow as the world diminishes. And your grief and your anguish will increase as human suffering around you increases. And you will feel helpless and hopeless regarding your position in the universe, for you have not found the power of Knowledge yet to redeem you.

This is the consequence of living at a time of Revelation. It is not just a matter of choosing this over that. It is not one teaching versus another teaching. It is the crucial thing that will make all the difference. Success and failure here are utterly consequential for the individual, for you.

This is why people think that Revelation cannot happen again because they really do not want to deal with the challenge and the opportunity and the re-evaluation it will require and present. Better to live with old Revelations that have been well established, where human commentary has overlaid them so completely that it is hard to really understand what the Revelations were talking about in the first place.

They [the old Revelations] have become the establishment. They have become the institution. They have become the accepted norm. There are individuals who recognize their true value and attempt to live this value. But for most people this is simply what is expected of them in their culture and nation—to believe and to follow, to some degree at least, but never with great seriousness or real devotion.

So into this compromised environment, God has spoken again and sent a Messenger into the world, sent from the Angelic Presence and Host to deliver a new reality, to shake people out of their complacency, to call people out of the shadows of their past, to bring clarity and resolution where there is only opinion and speculation, to take people beyond belief and their intellectual understanding to a greater reality of recognition and redemption.

If you can understand the origin of the Messenger, you will begin to understand your origin and what has called you into the world, which is an entirely different way of looking at your life—your present life, your past life and your future—and indeed a remarkable way of looking at the world. For there will be no condemnation here, only recognition and determination and great compassion for humanity as it struggles to find its real strength at a time of Revelation.

CHAPTER 3

THE LINEAGE OF THE MESSENGER

As revealed to
Marshall Vian Summers
on November 16, 2012
in Boulder, Colorado

To present God's New Revelation in the world, a Messenger has been sent, prepared to carry the burden of a New Revelation, bringing a new reality into the world.

This happens once perhaps in a thousand years as humanity reaches a great threshold—a turning point in its evolution and a time of great and immense challenge, not for merely one tribe or group but for all of humanity.

People everywhere are beginning to realize that they are approaching this threshold—a time of environmental decline, a time of great change in the world's climate, a time of economic and political upheaval, a time when the risk of great war is upon humanity over who will have access to the remaining resources of the world, a time when nations are unable to take care of their citizens and to provide for them adequately, a time when humanity faces intervention from aggressive and invasive forces from the universe who seek to claim dominance here without the use of force.

It is perhaps the greatest turning point in human history, for it will affect the outcome for all people, of all nations and faith traditions.

It [the Revelation] is not merely to introduce a new reality to one people, nation or group, for it is here now to speak to the whole world—a world now that has global communication and commerce, a world now that has very little time to prepare for the great change that is coming to the world.

The Messenger is sent from the Angelic Host. There is only one, for there can be only one, for there is only one who was prepared to receive a Revelation from God and to bring it into the world and to carry it there.

He is a man without position in the world. He is a humble man. He is a man who has proven he has the character, the faith and the compassion and commitment to carry such a great burden and gift.

It has taken 40 years for the Messenger to receive and prepare for the Revelation. It is a process of great mystery and power, a process that no one on Earth can really understand completely. It is an engagement with the Divine. It is where God once again gives a warning, a blessing, preparation and direction to the human family.

It comes from a great Lineage, from those who stand with the Messenger in this greater purpose. This is what brings resonance and unity and shows that the Revelation itself is part of an ongoing process—the next stage, the next great directive, the next great step for the human family as it stands at the threshold of space and as it faces a declining world, a world now polluted and degraded from human ignorance, abuse and misuse.

Those who stand with the Messenger represent the great traditions of the world—the Buddha, the Jesus and the Muhammad, previous Messengers who have brought great change and direction to build human civilization, to bridge the borders of cultures and nations to bring a greater spiritual awareness and practice into the world.

The Messenger now carries on their tradition, and they stand with him. For he is representing their will and the purpose that guided them, which guides him now.

This must be emphasized or people will think that this is somehow a contradiction or a competition, that it stands in conflict with their tradition and the traditions of the world when, in actuality, it is the perfect next step, you see.

For human civilization has been established. Though it is fragile and full of corruption and difficulty, it has been established. There is world community now and interdependence. There is world awareness, to a certain degree. There is even world compassion and conscience, to a certain degree. It [human civilization] is far from perfect, and it is fragile in a changing world. It can be undermined by intervention from without and by collapse from within.

That is why God has spoken again. For God will continue to direct the human family as long as it shows promise to become a free and self-determined race in a universe where freedom is rare and must be established and maintained with great care and vigilance.

The Lineage of the Messenger is the Lineage of all the Messengers, and of those who have sent all the Messengers, who are the same and the One—the Assembly of the Angelic Host assigned to oversee the world, this one world amongst innumerable worlds in the universe.

Wherever intelligent life has evolved or has planted itself in its latter stages of technological development, an Angelic Presence is there.

This is the theology of God's Work in the universe, which is for the first time being presented through the New Message for humanity.

To understand what God is doing in the world, you must have an understanding now of what God is doing throughout this Greater Community of life in the universe. And for the first time in history, this is now being presented.

It is all part of God's Plan, you see, set in motion at the beginning of time, set in motion at the beginning of human civilization, set in motion and now being carried forth in its next stage of evolution and development.

For this is not the end of the world. These are not the end times. This is a great transition, and for this transition to be successful and not disastrous, humanity must be prepared for living in a new world of environmental and economic restraint.

Humanity must be prepared to engage wisely with a universe of intelligent life, a non-human universe [that] is now intervening in the world in certain ways—ways that humanity is unaware of or does not understand, ways that are a direct threat to human sovereignty and the future of human freedom here on Earth.

It is a momentous time to be in the world at a time of Revelation. But the meaning of Revelation and the process of Revelation must be clearly understood, or you will not be able to recognize the great meaning of this time and what it means for you and how you are connected to it and what it reveals about your life and greater purpose being in the world at this time, with all its great global problems and human tragedies.

If you are a Christian, you must realize that Jesus stands by the Messenger. For Jesus will not return to the Earth, but is now overseeing humanity's emergence into this Greater Community of life.

For you who are Buddhist, you must realize the Buddha stands with the Messenger. For he [the Messenger] brings a greater inner awareness, and he brings the preparation to engage with humanity's deeper nature, with him now in a form and in a way that can be studied everywhere, for all people of all faith traditions.

For you who are a Muslim, you must realize that the Prophet Muhammad stands with the Messenger. For he [the Messenger] continues the great work of building and protecting human civilization, now facing a set of problems and challenges never before seen in the world.

All of these great Messengers from the past realize that their traditions cannot prepare humanity for what is to come and for what is here already, and for what must be done and undone, and changed and realized and brought into being.

For the great traditions of the past cannot prepare humanity for living in a new world, where great compassion and cooperation will have to be established if humanity is to survive in a world of diminished resources, violent weather and environmental change.

Here there cannot be competition between the religions of the world. There cannot even be competition between the nations of the world if humanity is to be provided for and made safe and secure in a turbulent world, where there will be great uncertainty and upheaval.

So We have reached the point in the great timeline of humanity's evolution where a New Revelation must be given. The need for this was foreseen long ago by those who watch over the world.

It is no accident that you are here or have reached this great turning point. It is no mishap or by mere chance that this has happened, for all races in the universe who develop technologically will reach a point where they will deplete their own planet's provisions and will have to face the reality of the Greater Community itself.

The Lineage of the Messenger means that he stands in harmony with all the great traditions—not as people interpret them, not as they have become altered and changed on the landscape of the world, not as they have been altered and misconstrued by governments and institutions and ambitious individuals seeking to use the Revelations for their own advancement and their own personal goals.

This is why God's New Message will have all the great traditions of the world reassessing their fundamental beliefs and assertions because you are emerging into a Greater Community of life. You are now dealing with a God of a billion, billion, billion races and more. You are facing a non-human universe where human ethics and where human values will not be shared or even recognized.

You are facing a world now that will require, out of necessity, great human cooperation and great giving and compassion from peoples everywhere, from all faith traditions—superseding and overshadowing theological debates and contention over who the Messengers were, and which religion is better or more true to God's Plan and Will.

You are living at a time of Revelation, as important as any time of Revelation in the past. And you are here bearing witness to the

Revelation, which could never occur in the past beyond a local community of people.

You are now hearing the Voice of Revelation—a Voice such as spoke to the Jesus, the Buddha and the Muhammad; the Voice not of one individual but of all the Angelic Host together.

It is a time of Revelation for those who can respond. It is a time of calling and great meaning and confirmation for those who can respond. But to respond, you must understand what you are looking at here. You must recognize the importance of the Messenger in the world. And you must understand that all God's Messengers stand with him in his great purpose and mission here on Earth.

This will require that you understand that God is the Source of all the world's true religions. They all began with a Divine purpose and intent. And they have all been changed and altered over time.

But now God's New Revelation is pure. You are even hearing the Voice of Revelation. You are hearing the words that were spoken, words so similar to those spoken to the Jesus, the Buddha and the Muhammad and all the great saints and humanitarians over time who have contributed to the well-being of humanity, and who have helped to build a human civilization where Knowledge has been kept alive, where the spiritual reality has been kept alive.

Humanity has not destroyed itself already because of the power and the presence of this Knowledge and this awareness in enough people. And great works and giving have occurred throughout time because of the power of this presence and awareness.

But now humanity's survival and the survival of human civilization itself are at great peril, a greater peril now than has ever existed—

greater than the world wars of the past century, greater than any threat or challenge.

For there are others who seek domination of the world, and they will seek to achieve their goals without the use of force. They will seek not to destroy humanity but to harness humanity for their own purposes. They realize the value of the Earth and that it is being despoiled by human greed, ignorance, competition and conflict. And they will intervene to preserve these things—the world's value and resources—for their own needs and use.

But humanity can preserve the world for itself and for its future and for the well-being of all people. But it will require a great change in awareness and understanding, a great and different understanding of God and God's Work in the world, and how God redeems individuals and entire worlds through the power and presence of Knowledge that has been placed within each person.

It is a new threshold, a new education, but one that is entirely natural and intrinsic to who you are and to the peoples of the world. For God loves humanity and understands humanity's plight and dilemma and the cause of human error and misunderstanding.

That is why God has placed Knowledge within each individual, waiting to be discovered. For it is this that will redeem the individual and bring them back to the Divine connection and awareness, leading them to act in harmony with others and to give their gifts to a world whose needs are escalating with each passing day.

It is the great challenge of Revelation. It is the great gift of Revelation. It is the great time in which God has spoken again, giving humanity, all of humanity now, a great chance to see, to know and to act in harmony with itself; to serve a world in need; to prepare for a difficult future and to safeguard human unity, sovereignty and freedom in this world amidst the presence of other opposing forces.

This will have all the world's religions reassessing their fundamental beliefs, and all the believers of religions reconsidering how they are responding to God's Presence and Work in the world.

It will be a great challenge, but a redeeming one at that. For here, one group is not set against another. Here no one is demeaned and denied. Here no religion is disputed and discarded. Here no people are forgotten or misused. Here the great Love of God, the great Compassion of God, and the great Wisdom of God are fully brought into Revelation—not for one group or one people, but for all of humanity.

To realize these things, to see these things and to realize the great truth that they represent, you must come to the Revelation. You must read it and hear it and study it and begin to apply it in your life and circumstances.

You must have the humility to set aside your grievances, your admonitions and your fixed beliefs in order to receive the blessings of the Creator—given now for you with such power and clarity, given so completely that it does not require human commentary or human explanation. For it is the largest Revelation ever given to this world, and it is given at a time where humanity is literate, where there is a world community and a world communication.

It is not a refutation of the past, but a confirmation of the past. But to see this, you must have a new understanding of God's Plan and Purpose for the peoples of this world and why God is preparing humanity for the Greater Community of life, which it must now face, and why God is preparing humanity to restore the world so that it may continue to support human civilization and the well-being of people everywhere.

For this, you must have clear eyes, for God's New Revelation will refute much of human understanding, belief and assertions, for these are born of ignorance—past ignorance and present ignorance. These are born of misunderstanding and misinterpretation.

For now you are hearing the Voice that spoke to the Buddha, the Jesus and the Muhammad. And God's Revelation is telling you that these three great Emissaries stand with the Messenger for this time and the times to come.

For there is only one Messenger in the world, and he represents those who sent him and those who stand with him. He is bringing the Word of God into the world for the first time in over 1400 years—for the first time. This is it.

It is not a question of belief. It is a question of recognition, honesty and humility and the willingness to receive. This is the challenge for the recipient.

There is no condemnation in God's New Revelation. There is no judgment against humanity. There is no cruel punishment awaiting those who cannot respond. There is no claiming that everyone must believe in one thing only, for this can never be the case. God knows this. There can never be a one-size-fits-all religion, for this will never work. And God understands this.

That is why the Revelation given gives such power to the individual and opens the way for personal revelation, which would be very difficult to achieve in the traditions of the past, given how they have been misused and misconstrued over time by people.

The Jesus, the Buddha and the Muhammad stand with the Messenger, for he is continuing their great work in the world, a great work that they hold in harmony with one another.

For they all in truth and in clarity represent the one Purpose, the one Will and the one Plan of God: to develop human conscience, human ethics and human civilization; to prepare humanity for a greater future within this world and within the Greater Community of worlds; to preserve and build human freedom over time and to build compassion, acceptance, forgiveness and humility so that human civilization will be truly beneficial and truly sustaining for the human family here on Earth.

CHAPTER 4

THE STORY OF THE MESSENGER

As revealed to
Marshall Vian Summers
on May 23, 2011
in Boulder, Colorado

Today We shall tell the story of the Messenger. It is a story that holds great power and meaning if it can be comprehended.

For the Messenger is no ordinary person, though he appears to be ordinary on the outside. And because he is a humble man, he does not exalt himself in any way. He seeks not recognition, but a deeper connection with those who are destined to meet him and to receive God's New Revelation.

In this sense, he is understated and will remain silent with others. His proclamation is not of himself, but of the Revelation, for that is why he has come. That is his reason for being in the world.

However, for most of his life so far, he was not aware of this. For his calling came later in life at a time when he was prepared to receive it and to begin the long preparation that would be required to prepare to receive the Revelation, and then to receive the Revelation itself.

Forty years it would take to do all of this. Forty years of being available, of treading the wilderness without a certain outcome, without realizing the significance of his endeavor. Forty years without other serious obligations beyond his family. Forty years to develop the trust and the confidence and the allegiance and the integrity that would be needed to become the Messenger.

Before he was sent into the world, the Angelic Host prepared him and placed deep within his mind the awareness and the understanding that he would later bring into the world—Knowledge and Wisdom from the universe, from the most advanced races in the universe; an understanding of the future of the world and where humanity is heading in its evolution, and all of the great hazards and risks associated with this; a greater understanding of human relationships that would give him a greater maturity as he would grow up in the world.

These are all placed deep within him, beneath the surface of the mind—later to be discovered, later to emerge and later to resonate with the Revelation itself. For the Revelation would not be foreign to him because of what has been given to him before he came into the world.

He was sent to a family, a conservative family, living in America, a family that would have no notion of his greater destiny and greater comprehension. There he would grow up with a minimum of influences from the world, insulated and sheltered from the tragedies and corruption of the world around him. He would grow up in a family with two older brothers and with an ill father, a father who would otherwise have had undue influence upon him. It was setting the stage for something in the distant future to emerge.

He would go through school, graduate from the university, and the only awareness he would have is that he had a greater and very unusual destiny and purpose in the world. He was restrained from giving himself to any career or to any relationship, restrained from committing his life before the Revelation could occur.

During this period, he would learn a great deal about the condition of the world and about human relationships. He would meet many people, and taste the sorrows and pleasures of this world to a certain extent, but always being withheld for something greater.

For this, he would have to develop trust that his life was not being lost or wasted. And the Presence was only with him to the extent that it could maintain his true direction and aim his life towards the sacred rendezvous that would happen much later.

When he was [32] years old, We presented Ourselves to him, and the initiation began—an initiation that would alter everything about his life. And yet because of who he was and what had been given to him, the resonance would be there. Our presence and Our purpose would not be foreign to him—only shocking and new and uncertain.

Later he would meet his great partner, his wife, who would journey with him through all the difficult and formative years that would be required for him to prepare for his greater role in life. His son would emerge soon thereafter, and he too would have a greater destiny with his father.

Others would come to join him as he began his long preparation. Not all of them would be able to stay with him, however. Some would falter and fail by the wayside or could only provide support for a very short time. Yet his true companions would begin to arrive as he would make progress in his preparation.

When he was 40 years old, he was given the Steps to Knowledge, the great Teaching of the Revelation, the Book of Practices. And he would be prepared to receive this in a very short time, under extraordinary circumstances. This would begin another stage in his preparation to be the Messenger.

But even at this age, he would not yet know of his destiny and his future role. For these things cannot be revealed too soon, or the person can become terrified or overwhelmed and withdraw or seek escape. So the realization of his destiny and his significant role in the world would only be given incrementally as he made progress.

During this time, he tried to have others be with him in his inexplicable journey, but few could join him beyond his wife and son and a few other individuals. For who can travel the road of Mystery and maintain their health and well-being and stability in the world in the process?

For Marshall to be able to become the Messenger, he would have to have a foot in both worlds—a foot in the real world of human interactions, human relationships, and the difficulties and complexities of relations between nations. He would have to see things that were very troubling. He could not hide in a preferential world, believing in only happy things or beautiful things or spiritual things.

He would have to have a foot in the Mystery, deeply anchored there so that the challenges and the temptations of the future would not take him out of his role and purpose.

Who in the world can understand these things? Who in the world has ever met the Messenger or can comprehend the mystery and the power of his presence in the world?

Many people will simply want things from the Messenger—miracles, dispensations, favors. They want to be healed. They want to be blessed. They want to be enriched. They want to be rescued. They want to be saved. They do not care who he is as long as he can provide these things, and then they will believe, but only to receive, you see.

His journey, therefore, would be lonely, isolated, beyond the range of even those who were sent to accompany him and to assist him.

He would have to live in two worlds, bridging two realities—so very unlike each other they are. Who can do this without losing their mind, or falling apart, or being seduced by darker forces in the world, or being overtaken by tragedy and loss and deprivation? It has been a very long road to travel, a very challenging road with many hazards, but the Messenger has arrived at his destination.

It has taken him [over] 25 years to receive the Revelation, it is so great. It is the largest Revelation ever given to this world because the world is [now] a literate world, a world of human communities and a world community, a world of global transportation, global infrastructure and communications.

Here you are not preparing to live some sweet pastoral life somewhere. You are preparing for a world in decline, a world of diminishing resources and growing economic and political upheaval. And you are facing the reality of life in the universe—a reality that poses hazards, dangers and opportunities that humanity has not yet recognized.

These are things that the Messenger has been prepared to speak on, for they are part of the Revelation, as they are part of humanity's destiny—a destiny that few in the world can yet see clearly without distortion or personal preference.

The Messenger appears ordinary. He is a humble man. He will not assert himself personally. But within him is the Mystery and the Power of Creation, and the bridge between this world and the Divine Presence that oversees this world.

He is partly one of Us and partly one of you. He has to maintain both realities and be the shepherd to lead people up the mountain that is their mountain to climb.

Is he as great as the great Emissaries of the past? Only time and circumstance will tell. He will not proclaim this himself, you see, because the ambitious are never chosen. Those who seek self-glorification are never given greater roles to play or greater Messages for humanity. Only those who are reluctant and honest and self-reflective would ever be chosen for such a high and significant role.

For there is only one Messenger in the world, and this Messenger will be the Messenger for this time and the times to come. No one else asserting this for themselves can bring the Revelation. No one else can travel the journey that the Messenger has had to travel.

Others will give important gifts where they are needed, and ultimately everyone is meant to do this, for that is part of each person's purpose. Everyone will be a conduit for a greater Presence and Power. But there is only one Messenger, whose Message will alter the course of human understanding and speak of the great change that will change the course of human destiny and evolution.

Without the New Message from God, humanity would fall into grave conflicts and precipitous decline, making you vulnerable to foreign powers who are already in this world to gain influence and authority here. People do not realize they are standing at the precipice, not only of great change but also of subjugation.

This is the Greater Darkness in the world, a Greater Darkness that most people are too afraid to even think about. But it is something that humanity must prepare for, and that is why God has given a New Revelation.

THE STORY OF THE MESSENGER

A new Prophet has come into the world. Judge him as you may. Exalt him or deny him. Call him great or call him other things. People's estimation has nothing to do with the reality. For what people want and what God knows are not the same. What people think and where the world is going are not the same.

The Messenger will be denied. He will be ridiculed. Others will attack him. Others will feel threatened by his presence and his proclamations—not because he is wrong but because they cannot face the fact that God has spoken again. They do not have the courage or the humility to reconsider their position, their ideas or their previous investment in themselves.

This is the challenge of meeting the Messenger. He brings a whole new reality with him, in him, around him and through him—a reality that humanity is not yet mature enough to face collectively. Only individuals will be ready for him, for they have been made ready through their life experience, through disillusionment and disappointment and other things.

There are many people waiting for the New Revelation. They must know of the Messenger, for he is the demonstration that the Power and the Presence has come back into the world.

To see this, you must look with clear eyes. You must listen. You must listen with a deeper listening. You must allow the power of Knowledge, the deeper intelligence within you, to respond.

For if you judge the Messenger based upon ideas or your own projections of fear and blame, you will not see and you will not know.

If you cannot receive God's New Revelation, then what can God really do for you? If you cannot follow what God has put within you to follow, the power and the presence of Knowledge, what else can God do for you or the world?

There are countless worlds in the universe, inhabited worlds. This is only one. The Lord of this world is the Lord of all worlds. It is not a human universe you are facing, and that is why your notions of Heaven and Hell are so incorrect, so limited and really pathetic. It is to take you into the Greater Community that represents part of the purpose of the Messenger and of the New Revelation.

The Messenger is facing a monumental task. He alone cannot bring the Revelation into the world. It will require the participation, the contribution and the communication of many others who can assist him in this way.

The Revelation has been given with its own commentary and in such great detail and repetition that it will not rely so greatly upon human interpretation as have the previous Messages that have been given to humanity. It brings with it the understanding of spirituality at the level of Knowledge; Knowledge and Wisdom from the Greater Community; a preparation for a new and declining world; a great teaching on human relationships and responsibility and what nations must know to cooperate with one another in the face of the great change that is coming.

This is not one man's philosophy. This is beyond philosophy. This is not associated with any world religion. This is the beginning of a whole new understanding. This is not a rejection or reaction to the world's religions. This is a New Message from God.

The Messenger is in the world. He will not be in the world for a long, long time to come, and that is why he must be recognized, for those who have this great opportunity.

His life has been inexplicable. His presence is inexplicable. You must see with clear eyes and listen with a deeper hearing to recognize these things. The burden, then, is upon the listener, upon the recipient.

The Messenger has received almost the entire communication. It is enough to last for generations and centuries. For no one can tell you how to prepare for the new world. No one can tell you how to prepare for a Greater Community of intelligent life—a competitive environment on a scale you cannot even imagine. No one can tell you of the deeper mind. No one can provide the New Revelation.

The Revelations are always given to one individual, so there is no confusion. There are no different versions. There is no competition between different individuals who make the same claim and proclamation. It is always one individual with the assistance of certain courageous people that can bring a new awareness and reality into the world.

Every age has its prophets, but the Messengers only come infrequently to alter the course of human understanding, awareness and destiny.

You will see that the Messenger will be judged. He will be condemned. Others will make it their purpose to destroy him. Learn the lessons from the past in this regard. He is not simply here to sacrifice himself so that other people can create a story about him. He has his own story—the story of the Messenger, a story he is too humble to speak of, a story that must be revealed to all who can hear and understand.

People want the Messenger to be many things, to meet their desires, their beliefs and their preferences. But the Messenger has been prepared by Greater Powers and sent from the Divine to be in the world according to a Greater Plan and destiny.

Be careful, then, in how you approach this rare and significant individual. Be careful regarding your expectations, your beliefs, your preconceived ideas, your judgments and your grievances. For these can all blind you to who he is and to what he can offer to you and to the whole world.

May the Blessing be with him. The Power and the Presence is with him.

He is fallible. He is not perfect. He will face many difficulties. It is what is in him and with him and through him that is perfect. His life is a vehicle for this, as your life is a vehicle for something important as well. But he is the seed of a greater future for humanity, a new understanding of your existence within a Greater Community of life and of the great turning point that humanity is now beginning to undergo.

Let this be your understanding. But do not come to conclusions, for the awareness of the Messenger is only just beginning.

CHAPTER 5

THE REQUIREMENTS OF THE MESSENGER

As revealed to
Marshall Vian Summers
on March 12, 2013
in Boulder, Colorado

Surely, one who is called and prepared to bring a New Message from God into the world must have a long and very challenging preparation. It is the preparation an individual could not initiate for themselves.

It must be a calling from Heaven itself. It must be administered by Heaven itself. It must take the one chosen from their former life and state of mind into a new life and a far greater state of mind over a period of time.

It is a preparation with many challenges and many tests. It is not a journey any individual could invent for themselves, for their own edification or self-proclamation, though many have tried, and certainly others in the future will try as well.

God's Messenger is no ordinary person. God's Messenger is not simply someone who was called out of the crowd and given an important task in life, or [asked] to carry an important message, like a postman. It is someone who must come from the Angelic Presence itself, and be initiated into the world, and be given time to develop as a human being facing the pleasures and the hazards and the disappointments of living in Separation.

It must be one of the Angelic Assembly who can do such a task. So never think that God's Messenger is simply some witless person who was chosen and burdened with a great and important mission. No, indeed. This individual would have to have unique qualities and a greater association to be able to assume such a pivotal and important role in life.

For here failure is incredibly damaging, not only to the one chosen but to all of humanity. For if the Message cannot be received correctly and interpreted and communicated correctly, then it will have been corrupted. It would be incomplete.

For, you see, the Message requires the Messenger, and the Messenger has to have the qualities necessary to carry out such a great and demanding task. If the individual does not have such qualities, then they cannot emanate the Presence. They cannot carry the burden. They will never be selfless enough to sacrifice their own needs and pleasures along the way. Invariably, if they were not chosen for such a task, they would not be able to complete such a mission.

Certainly, those who follow the Messenger, now and in the future, may be prone to misinterpret and misapply God's New Revelation for humanity. And sadly that will occur because people do not yet have the clarity and integrity and understanding yet to be able to carry such a Message forth beyond the time of the Messenger.

That is why certain people are chosen and selected to do this at the very center of the Messenger's life. They too must prepare and meet requirements. They too must follow an inexplicable journey not of their own making. They too must face great uncertainty and opposition in the world. They too must hold the vision and the Fire of Knowledge despite the chaos they see around them and the tragic nature of the human pursuit for happiness and fulfillment.

The requirements of the Messenger are very unique. And We give them to you now so that you may understand this person, that you might recognize what is required and recognize that only one is given the responsibility to receive and to initiate the proclamation of God's New Revelation. Once you understand the requirements, perhaps, you will be able to accept this yourself.

First, the Messenger, before he even knows he is the Messenger or has any idea of this, must be held back from giving his life away to people, places and things. He will need to be educated fundamentally, but he cannot commit himself to family and career until his moment of initiation occurs, which would be later in his life, beyond his early youth. Therefore, he must be restrained, and he must restrain himself. He must honor the feeling within himself to be restrained.

He must not become politically engaged. He must not become seriously socially engaged. He must not have radical views. He must be very healthy. He must grow up in a healthy family, but be able to move beyond that family and its obligations and expectations. He must not have any religious training, or be religiously oriented particularly, so that his ideas do not become preconceived and formulated early in life. He must respect religion, but not become closely tied to it in any form.

He will have to be willing to wait a very long time for his true partner and mate to arrive. And he must feel this and know this within himself sufficiently so as not to pursue romance or commitment in relationship before it is appropriate for him to do so.

He must not become an ardent spiritual practitioner, for this will set in train preconceived notions that would only have to be undone later. So it is better that he restrain himself and be restrained even from this.

His youth will be ordinary, but exceptional in some ways. He will not understand himself or his motivations, for that could not be understood at this early stage. He will have to trust a feeling that will only be there intermittently.

He will have to want things but not have them, without knowing why. While everyone around him is giving themselves over to people, places and things, he cannot do this.

He must learn about relationships, human passion and the follies of romance. He must see people committing all manner of errors and mistakes, without condemnation.

He must wait. That is so very important here to understand. For who can wait? Can you wait, really wait, for the time, for the moment?

When the Rays of Initiation would be shone upon him so powerfully, it would obliterate his former life and sever his connections, just enough so that he could be free to embark on a greater journey—a journey not of his own making, a journey that no one around him could understand, except perhaps the very wise.

He would have to study and train for this Initiation. He would have to begin to teach the inexplicable Teaching in The Way of Knowledge and begin to learn its fundamental and primary lessons.

He would have to be intelligent but yielding, capable but ready for something greater without knowing what it is, what it is for or where it would take him.

At his moment of great Initiation, he would have to be able to maintain his internal composure and to follow the directives that would certainly arise from such a monumental encounter, an encounter that few people in the world have ever had at this level of intensity.

Only the Jesus, the Buddha and the Muhammad have been struck in this manner. For they too have come from the Angelic Assembly, as has the Messenger for this time and for this world.

People can claim any title they want. They can assume anything. They can believe anything. They can imagine anything. But only Heaven knows who is to receive a preparation of this nature, and for what purpose, and for what ultimate end.

The Messenger then would have to begin to unravel his former life, to leave his relationships and to embark on a period of wandering. For nine months, he wandered, not knowing what he was doing, not knowing where he was going, with just enough money to support him during this period.

He would have to go where he was meant to go. He would have to not engage himself seriously in any relationship. He [would have to not] run away, and try to be safe anywhere or secure or loved or protected. With a greater destiny, he cannot give himself to these things.

At the end of nine months, We came upon him again and told him to begin to prepare to record, which he did. And that began, very early, the transmission of God's New Revelation. Yet it would be a long time before he would know what it was for, why it was even occurring, for there was no assurance at the beginning.

He was not given his role at the beginning, for he would have to prove himself now, again and again. For seven years, he would have to prove himself and prepare to receive the Angelic Presence, which he could only do for moments at a time at the outset.

He would have to record. He would have to provide Our testimony to certain people.

He would have to move his family around repeatedly to certain places that were important for him to experience, to learn of the Greater Community and of the more hidden powers working in the world today, both for and against humanity.

His partner would arrive, and his son soon after. He would be a father and a husband and have to be responsible in all ways here, but still being guided by a mysterious Light, without a certain outcome or destiny. For these things would not be revealed to him until much, much later.

He would have to be strong emotionally. He would have to be stable. He would have to be dependable and reliable, day in and day out, and build his strength in this way, as well as his deeper connection to those who sent him here.

He would receive entire teachings. He would begin to lay the foundation, brick by brick, of the greatest Revelation ever given to humanity—beginning with people's personal realms, beginning the teaching on how to receive a Revelation and to learn over time how to live it and to share it with others.

After seven years, he would receive Steps to Knowledge, the book of preparation in God's New Revelation. He would have to be able to receive the Assembly for long periods of time, for days on end, to receive this important teaching and preparation for humanity.

He would have to relocate to do this and leave his former home entirely, never to return, and take his family with him, along with others to assist him in this great endeavor.

From here, he would have to search for a future home for the Revelation. He would have to travel across the country again and again to find this place, for it cannot be merely told to him where to go. It must be experienced once he arrived. For he would have to take complete responsibility for his actions, even though he was being guided from above.

He could not claim the Angels of God were directing him, for he was not allowed to do this. He had to be responsible for everything, and take responsibility for the consequences, and be accountable for his actions. For only certain people would be allowed to know the real secret of his life.

He would have to go through the difficult process of establishing a home in an entirely new place—where he knew no one, had no associations and no family and no history—and there to begin to receive the great books of the Revelation, and to begin to call people to assist him.

But he was not yet ready to be a world teacher. He did not yet have these strengths or this comprehension. And he would have to wait many years for the Revelation to be given to him, step by step, and build itself into a world Teaching and ultimately a New Message from God. It would only be later that the true purpose and meaning of his long journey would be revealed to him.

He had to undergo illness and incapacity for long periods of time from the great strain of undertaking this journey.

He would have to call certain people to assist him. He would have to raise his son, who would become an important person in the Revelation, and in the future of the Revelation in this world.

Everyone around him would have to develop significantly, and not everyone would be able to do this. Certain people would fall away, yet others would stay with him faithfully. He would have great difficulties at this time of maintaining the beginning organization that would be responsible for transmitting and teaching God's New Revelation for the world.

He would have to build the qualities of discernment, restraint and discretion, stability, faith, confidence and the ability to deal with small problems at every turn, and the needs of others that were genuine. He would have to be a pillar of strength. Even at this time of great uncertainty for him, he would have to be a pillar of strength for others.

And all the while, his connection to the Assembly was growing, slowly, carefully, so as not to disable him from being able to be functional in the world, but to be a bridge between this world and the [spiritual] world beyond—strengthening his connection to each of these worlds and to the Beings that exist in each of these worlds.

Here he could not surrender himself to God and give up all worldly activities, for he would be building the seeds and the foundation for great world activities and a great participation in the world.

Here he would not become an ascetic and withdraw from life. He would be a husband and a father and a leader of an organization, all the while cultivating the great mystery of his life and purpose.

He would have to be responsible for everything he did and not reveal to others the Source of his guidance or the nature of the mystery of his life. Only his wife and son and a few others would know of these things.

He would have to develop his skills as a teacher, not just for individuals but for groups of people, for his destiny would be to speak to a whole world in the future.

He would have to be compassionate, wise and competent, careful and discerning, patient, oh so very patient, with himself and others.

He would have to develop inner listening so that he could hear and feel the power of Knowledge speaking as he was serving the needs of others.

He would have to let people come and go, for not everyone has the strength to undertake the preparation provided by God's New Revelation.

He would have to hold fast to his purpose and his direction through times of great emptiness when he would not hear from the Angelic Assembly. He would have to build his own strength based upon Knowledge within himself. For he would have to become the strong vehicle for something so great and profound that the world can barely understand it.

Through more periods of difficulty with his health, he would begin the proclamation and to receive the teachings of the proclamation, even the teachings about himself, as the New Message began to become fulfilled and complete through him.

He would have to be humble, knowing that this was beyond him and greater than him. And yet he would have to be confident that he could take the next step and not seek an escape, as so many people do.

His strength would have to be quiet. He would not declare himself. Only as the Revelation became complete would he begin to state its reality and have to admit that he really was the Messenger.

He would have to overcome his own reluctance, for only the reluctant are chosen. For the task is too great, too demanding, too uncertain and even too dangerous for people to choose wisely with real understanding.

He would have to cultivate the necessary abilities and refinements that Heaven would require. And this would take years and years and years, as it has taken for all the great Messengers. For no one, even if they are chosen, is ready at the outset.

It has taken the Messenger 30 years to do this, and even longer given his early preparation. No one who is ambitious or self-determined could do this, could follow such an inexplicable journey and exercise such great forbearance, patience and stability. They would fall apart easily, for they do not have the inner strength or the greater connections with life to undertake such a greater task.

He would have to be prepared to deal with the great difficulties of bringing the preparation to a world of great dissonance, fear, anger and distrust—where people are caught up in their beliefs and their admonitions, their failures and their pursuits of wealth and power.

Who amongst them can hear God speaking again, through this individual? They may study their religions. They may even become religious teachers or scholars or advocates, but who can hear when God will speak again? Who has the humility to reconsider their ideas and beliefs? Who can listen to the stirrings of their heart and not merely be fixated in their beliefs and convictions and all that they have invested in, building up their position in the world?

They would not receive the Messenger, who is the answer to their prayers. They would dispute him, condemn him and dismiss him, for they are not yet ready to receive him.

The discouragement, the disappointment, the projections of evil and blame upon the Messenger will be heaped upon him as he proceeds. Even now he stands at the threshold of an unwelcoming world, seeking those individuals who can respond, who are ready to be amongst the first to receive the reality that God has spoken again.

They will come from every country, every nation, every culture, one by one, not in great groups. Hoards of people will not rush to the Revelation. It will begin with a calling, a great calling that not only exists in the outer world, but that exists in the inner world as well. And they will have to have the courage and the trust and the wisdom to respond.

If they do not respond and cannot respond and meet the requirements of their own calling, which is far less difficult and demanding than the Messenger's, then the New Message may not build a hold or a footing in the world and be able to serve the world at this time as it is meant to do.

For humanity is at the verge of failure—destroying the world it lives in, falling into despair, falling into chaos, falling into endless war and conflict over who will have access to the remaining resources of the world.

So this is not a Revelation for some distant need, but for the immediate needs of people everywhere. For to live without the power of Knowledge is to live in great fear and uncertainty. It is to suffer.

The Messenger is here to relieve that suffering, to give people strength and power, and to reveal to them the Will of Heaven and the real nature of their spirituality and greater calling in the world, and what the world will really need from them, beyond what they themselves may want to give for their own happiness.

He is at this threshold now of calling out individuals around the world, for this is a Teaching for the whole world and not merely for one tribe, one nation, one region or one group. And timing is critically important because the Message is given for the world now. It is not something to be merely studied in a casual manner, or considered over time, or disputed and debated in the halls of academia, where Knowledge is so very rare.

This is an urgent Message for humanity. The time is now. The need is overarching and growing with each passing day. Humanity cannot see or know what it must do. Not enough people have the conviction of heart to do what is really necessary. They must be reached by the Revelation. They can remain as Christians and Buddhists and Muslims, but they must be reached by the Revelation—enough people in the world.

So the Messenger is under tremendous pressure to do this with very limited resources and support. He is always dealing with uncertainty, you see, and a great challenge. He cannot live a life of repose. He cannot lose himself in meditation for long periods of time. For he is called to a great service in the world, whose needs are profound and growing every day. And he is the one who has God's answer.

This is where his strength, his patience and his determination really are needed and required, or he would break down and fall apart. He would give himself to some wild and inappropriate avenue to seek, or be seduced by others who would want to use him and his Revelation for their own self-importance and ideas.

No one understands the life of the Messenger. But We give these things to you so that you may begin to have an appreciation for who this individual is and what they have had to do and the long journey they have had to take. You who are impatient for everything cannot imagine the patience this has required and the forbearance it has required and the strength and responsibility it has required.

God wants you to understand the process of Revelation. God wants you to understand the life of the Messenger, if you can. God wants you to feel this with your heart and not merely discern it with your ideas.

God wants you to know the importance of the Revelation and what it has taken to bring it into the world, for the Messenger and for those who have abided with him and journeyed with him for so very long, during the long periods where he would have to remain in obscurity—preparing, building, studying.

These are the saints of the Revelation, not because they were so glowingly magnificent, but because of what they were able to do, and the fidelity that they demonstrated, and the courage and commitment that moved their lives.

See this in contrast to everyone and everything around you, and you will begin to see the power and the meaning of this for your life. For you too have a greater destiny and purpose and can learn from the life of the Messenger. But you are not called to do what he is called to do. You were not sent into the world to do what he was sent into the world to do, but to assist him and others in simple and humble ways but with a great spirit, the great strength and patience that the Messenger has demonstrated so far.

Heaven looks upon him with great appreciation, but also with great need. Heaven looks upon his wife and his son as key to his success. Heaven looks upon those called to the Revelation with great intention, for they are important now, more important than they even know or realize.

It is the Will of Heaven that God's Message be given to the world in a timely manner, to prepare enough people to face the great change that is coming to the world and humanity's encounter with life in the universe, a reality that no one in the world understands today.

That is why God has revealed as part of the Revelation the reality and spirituality of life in the universe. God has revealed the Great Waves of change that are coming to the world so that people may be alerted and informed and given this greater perspective, which will bring greater clarity, purpose and meaning to their lives and activities.

God does not prepare you for Heaven alone. God prepares you to deal with the real world and the New World that is coming that very few people in the world can yet see.

You too must have the humility to receive the Revelation. You must have the strength and perseverance to take the Steps to Knowledge. You must have the courage to live with questions that cannot yet be answered. You too must live the calling that extends far beyond your intellect and your understanding. You too must build the Four Pillars of your life—the Pillar of Relationships, the Pillar of Work and Providership, the Pillar of Health and the Pillar of Spiritual Development—all the things the Messenger has had to do and has been doing for so long.

You will understand his life more completely as you take the journey yourself and see how really challenging it is, and how immensely rewarding it is, and how confounding it may be to your understanding and to your ideas of yourself. For its purpose is to take you beyond these things into a greater life, a greater service and a greater purpose in the world.

The Messenger is in the world now. He is an older man. It would be a great honor and blessing for you to meet him during his life and to learn of him and to hold in your heart his demonstration and to receive his gift of Revelation, which will give you the life you have always sought in other things.

Heaven blesses him and blesses all who can receive of him. He is a humble man. But in Heaven he is known, and he stands with those great Messengers who have blessed and guided humanity in the past.

CHAPTER 6

THE VEIL OF THE MESSENGER

As revealed to
Marshall Vian Summers
on December 7, 2012
in Boulder, Colorado

To bring a New Message from God in the world requires a person who is uniquely designed for this greater mission, a person whose origin and destiny are distinct from everyone around him, a person whose preparation even before coming into this world is unique and very focalized. This is the person who will have to meet great expectations, the expectations of Heaven itself.

In order for this to be achieved, this individual will have to meet certain requirements and pass certain tests. For when anyone enters the world, they enter the world of influences. They enter a world of difficulty—a world of survival, a world of social acceptance, a world of challenges, a world where you will be unknown and unrecognized, except perhaps in a certain way by your family. But even here your greater purpose and mission will, in almost all cases, be unknown even to those who raise you and who grow up with you.

A great Messenger is now in the world, but he is hidden, you see. He is hidden behind an invisible veil—a veil of normalcy, a veil of ordinariness, a veil of simplicity. He is not an individual who will stun and amaze everyone around him. He will walk amongst the people and be unrecognized in the crowd, just another person. Interesting perhaps in certain respects, but not outstanding in any way that most people recognize.

In this regard, he is like all the other Messengers, who were very ordinary looking, who could disappear in a crowd. In spite of all the stories, miracles and wonderment that surround the earlier Messengers in ancient times, they were very ordinary looking people. They did not amaze and stun everyone who saw them. Perhaps they were confounding, and they were certainly different, particularly as their greater role began to emerge. Then they became really distinct.

It would still be a very difficult task for them to proclaim their Message, to communicate it effectively and to take the journey that would be spread out before them—a journey of great difficulty, a journey where they would be misunderstood and their words be misapplied, a journey of confusion, a journey without a map, a journey without a clear pathway, where they would have to find their way in the wilderness of this world, surrounded by society and what everyone does, a wilderness of confusion and paradox, set on a unique course of tremendous importance and high expectations from those who sent them into the world—a journey where failure would have immense consequences, not only for the Messengers, but for thousands and millions of people in their time and beyond.

Who can carry such a burden? Who can meet such a requirement? Who can follow such an inexplicable pathway and take a journey that no one else around them is taking or can take?

For this, they would have to be ordinary in appearance. Otherwise, society would try to use them. People would praise them. People would want things from them. They would be seduced by society and culture. The seductions of beauty, wealth and charm would interfere with their preparation, which would be long and remarkable. It would pull them into some kind of other role, far beneath them and far outside their true domain.

No one can really fully understand the role and the journey of the Messenger. And this is true today, for the reality of this does not change except in the appearance of things.

A New Messenger is in the world, carrying a New Message from God. He has had to walk this long and inexplicable journey, a journey of ever-growing responsibility and burden, for much of it without knowing the meaning, the purpose and the outcome of the path [he] would have to take, which would set [him] apart from everyone else, a journey not of amazement and wonderment alone, but of increasing challenge and the great weight of responsibility.

So the Messengers have to be veiled, or people will think they are something else and use them for something else, and give them accord, which is incorrect and improper.

For the Messenger to develop, he has to be able to walk in the world, unrecognized, to witness the world, to experience the mundanity and the tragedy of life and living in Separation.

Though he would be protected in a unique way and guided to a great extent, there would be long periods where those who sent him into the world would seem to be missing or vacant—alone, following an inexplicable light, a subtle calling that he hears only from time to time and that others do not hear, except for the rare few who are meant to join him and assist him. They can hear the calling too, but they do not know what it means or where it will take them or its greater significance for the future.

How different this is from the stories of the great teachers, the great Messengers of the past who have been glorified and even deified, whose every action is filled with significance and wonder, who seem to impress inordinately everyone around them, who seem to demonstrate extraordinary abilities, virtues and qualities, even in their youth. People cannot understand how they were veiled and why they had to be veiled to learn about life, suffering, joy and simplicity.

For, you see, the Messenger has to be simple. He cannot be filled with pride and self-importance. He cannot think of himself as above and beyond everyone else. And so the majority of his early life is mundane and unexceptional.

The Messenger has to be humble, for he has to bow to the mission given to him, and to those who have given it to him and to the Lord of all the universes, who has sent it to this individual to give to a world in need—a world that will not readily accept his presence or his proclamation.

Someone driven by pride and arrogance would quickly fail here and become embittered and vengeful, condemning the world. But the Messenger cannot do this. This would disqualify the Messenger, you see.

So here is the Messenger for this era and the times to come, bringing a Message that has not been brought into the world in over a millennium, a Message of such great importance, answering the needs of this time and of the times to come, bringing to people a reality that is beyond their current understanding and awareness, speaking of the life to come and what humanity must do to prepare for the great change that is coming to the world and for its encounter with a universe full of intelligent life.

His Message would have to be complete, expansive and inclusive, for he will be speaking to a world community now and not just to one tribe, one group or one region alone. He will be speaking to the whole world at once, not to his own culture or his isolated group.

His Message would have to be relevant to everyone and to all their circumstances—rich or poor, east or west, north and south. His mind would have to be expanded to encompass a Greater Community reality of life in the universe and a tremendous wisdom and compassion for humanity.

This would far exceed anything that the ancient Messengers ever had to conceive of. Yes, they were the true Messengers of their time. Yes, they were prepared for their journey and mission. Yes, they had to face all of the difficulties and lack of acceptance and recognition that their lives would bring to them.

But the Messenger today will have to carry a greater body of understanding, a greater capacity. He will be facing not only rejection from local authorities, but from an entire world of local authorities— challenging the religions of the world, challenging the assumptions of the world, challenging the complacency of people, challenging the direction of humanity and all of its self-comforting and self-assuring ideas, which could only be great hazards given the future of humanity.

This man, who is in the world, has no position. He is educated but not too educated. He is remarkable, but one must see beyond appearances to recognize this. It is his role and his proclamation and his gift that make him remarkable.

This has always been the case with all the Messengers, you see, and that is why their journey in part has been so difficult. They have had the most difficult tasks of anyone on Earth, but they have also been the most important people on Earth, certainly the most important people of their era and the eras to follow.

The importance that Heaven accords is not the importance that the Messenger will find in the world. He will be rejected. He will be denied. He will not meet people's expectations because of the veil, the veil of the Messenger—the veil of humility, the veil of appearing to be ordinary, the veil of vulnerability, the veil of simplicity.

It is what is in him and with him, his origin and his destiny, that set him in such a unique and important position. But to see this, one would have to recognize something, and hear his proclamation and receive the Revelation that is his to bring into the world. Only then, perhaps, could they begin to understand the burden of the Messenger and the journey of the Messenger. This could only be comprehended if they shared this journey, if they understood this journey from their own direct experience of the Message and the Messenger.

To everyone else, he is just some person making a big proclamation, some person who seems to have the arrogance to challenge their core and fundamental beliefs and expectations. He is not the superstar, the superhuman that they would expect a Messenger to be. He does not perform miracles right and left to impress the unknowing and to win the acceptance of those who could not accept him otherwise.

You cannot buy this recognition. You cannot purchase it. Even miracles will not garner it in truth. Therefore, the Jesus is misunderstood. The Buddha is misunderstood. The Muhammad is misunderstood—not only from the people of their time, but the people throughout time. It is their humility, their humanity, their surrendering, their preparation and the great difficulty and challenge of their journeys that really begin to reveal their remarkable nature, purpose and design.

You are blessed now to live at a time of Revelation; a time which only comes perhaps every thousand years; a time of great difficulty, challenge and change for the human family—now with humanity facing its greatest challenges of collapse and disintegration from within and intervention from without, facing now challenges never known before by humanity as a whole.

Into this grave and perilous time, God has sent a New Message for humanity to honor the world's religions and to create their common Source, to call out from people the greatness that they carry: the power of Knowledge that God has given to each person to guide them, to protect them and to lead them to a greater role in service in the world.

But God has sent a Messenger, too, who carries within him a part of the Message that is not in scripture, that has not been recorded, that has not been written. He is part of the Revelation, you see. But he is behind the veil. And you must look deeply and honestly to see beyond this veil.

He cannot be used to enrich people. He cannot be used to gratify people. He cannot be used to create a false sense of importance of the people around him. He cannot be used as a tool of the state. He cannot be used to enhance people's desire for wealth, power and charm.

Because he is veiled. You could sit next to him and perhaps not even notice, as many people have already. He could walk by you in the street, and you would take no notice that the most important person in the world just passed you, a person who has a gift for your life of such importance it cannot even be described.

There is only one Messenger for this time and the times to come because only one has been prepared, and only one has been sent.

Others may proclaim this title for themselves, but only Heaven knows who has been sent for this purpose.

To know him, you must hear him—his proclamation, the gift of Wisdom that passes through him: the Revelation from God brought into the world through one man who has carried such a great burden. It has broken him down emotionally. It has broken him down physically. It has endangered his health. It has given him a toil, an unseen and unrecognized toil.

It is not the toil of survival. It is not the toil of self-gratification. It is the toil of carrying a great Message that would have to remain unknown for a long time until the Messenger was ready to proclaim and to come forth with the Revelation that he had spent 30 years receiving.

You will be called to the Message and the Messenger, you and others. If you are called and cannot receive, you will become critical. You will become a critic—unable to break away, but unable to respond truthfully. You will become a critic, a detractor.

If you can respond, then your life will begin to change. If you can accept the pathway and take the Steps to the greater Knowledge within you that God has provided, then you will begin to prepare yourself for a greater life, and free yourself from your former existence and all that constrained you there.

If you have the opportunity to meet the Messenger in his remaining years on Earth, it would be a great blessing for you. But when you do meet him, you will see the veil. He will be a veiled person. He will not reveal what is within him. He will not show you what he sees about you and your life, except rarely, and only then if you were to become a true student of the Revelation. He will not answer your questions. He will not meet your needs. You cannot use him as a resource, though you may try.

His veil has protected him, has kept him pure in an impure world, has assured his humility and his strength. It has given him his humanity and his compassion and love for the human family. It has strengthened him to endure not only the great passage of receiving the Revelation, but the difficulty of presenting it to a world that is ambivalent about God and Creation, that lives for the moment and does not consider the future or the outcome of one's life, of people's lives.

The Messenger has to accept that he will go unrecognized and that his Message will not be appreciated by so many people. He will have to face the ridicule and the condemnation of those who are drawn but cannot receive. He will have to see the blind rejection of people who are attached to their philosophies, their theologies and their religious beliefs, who are blinded by their firm and fixed notions. They do not even recognize God's Emissary when he arrives on Earth. Even if they are religious, or consider themselves to be such, they cannot even recognize the Messenger.

The ignorance, the foolishness, the arrogance—the Messenger will have to face all of these without losing heart or becoming embittered. What compassion and restraint this requires, you can barely imagine. He who brings God's answer for humanity will see it despoiled and rejected, dismissed and ridiculed. But he cannot lose heart, and he cannot lose his compassion for humanity and his faith in humanity.

You who sit on the sidelines of life and who barely participate there can hardly imagine what it means to come into the world with such a gift and such a difficult task.

The Messenger is seeking certain people who will be amongst the first to respond. To everyone else, he must wait. He cannot be engaged there. He will call certain people to their greater purpose and destiny. And some of them will fail to respond. He will have to face ill health and lack of support all along the way because his journey has been so demanding.

All of this is the reality of the Messenger, hidden behind the veil of an ordinary appearance and a simple life. Here there are no grand self-assertions. Here there is no attempt to establish oneself as great and grand and significant. It is only the Message and the Proclamation that establish who he is, what he is and why he is here. He himself will not do this.

To be the focal point of so many people's adulation and hostility certainly is not a bright and happy prospect. To bring something pure and have it despoiled in the world is a heartwrenching prospect—to speak and not be heard; to give and have your gift not received; to speak to the needs of the people and have them turn away; to give the gift of promise, power, truth and integrity and have it discarded; to bring the one great Revelation into the world and have people think it is a mere teaching for their edification, a resource for them to use to enhance their beauty or their importance in the world.

Certainly no one wants to come into the world to have to do all this. What a thankless journey where one will be surely misunderstood and misconstrued. But the Messenger comes, and because he has been held back and because he has had to carry the burden for so long without recognition, he is humble, he is strong, he is without presumption.

He sees the folly of humanity. He sees the arrogance of humanity. But instead of condemning everyone and everything, he brings the gift that can restore people to their true power, stature and purpose in the world.

This is the veil of the Messenger, but it must also become your veil to a lesser extent as you learn to receive something pure and beautiful, and to be able to present it to the world without anger and condemnation, able to accept and face rejection, able to look for those who can receive and not malign those who cannot, able to take a journey not of your own making, but which has been prepared for you.

For all who will assist the Messenger and carry the Revelation into the world in its pure form will have to develop this veil, this power, this presence. They must be hidden too around certain people and certain places. They too must hold within their hearts the Fire of Knowledge and not let the world take it from them and exploit them. They too will have to comprehend the example of the Messenger, even far beyond his life, to see its demonstration, its relevance and importance for them and how they must learn to be in the world—a world of truth and folly, a world of misunderstanding and misconceptions. Here you do not need a hero to worship, but you do need an example to follow.

For to realize your greater purpose in the world, you must understand the things that We are speaking of here today. The life and the demonstration of the Messenger will help you, even though you are not asked to carry such a great burden or assume such a difficult and remarkable role.

It is the humility of the Messenger, and the strength and compassion of the Messenger that will bespeak his greater purpose, nature and role. If this can be recognized, its value to the individual, to you, will be immense, for these are things you are called to do. These are things you can do, and you must do, if you are to assume a greater life in service to a world in need.

This is part of the Messenger's gift to you, who are not merely a consumer of ideas, who will not merely use the Revelation as a resource for your own needs, but recognize your responsibility to help carry it forward in the world in its pure form, without wedding it or joining it with other things. Only then will you begin to fully understand the veil of the Messenger.

CHAPTER 7

UNDERSTANDING THE NEW MESSENGER

As revealed to
Marshall Vian Summers
on April 25, 2012
in Boulder, Colorado

Today We will speak on understanding the Messenger.

There are some people who will receive and welcome the idea of there being a New Message from God in the world. They see the need for this. They see how the old traditions have become fractured and contentious, both amongst themselves and within themselves. They see the religious extremism and its destructive impact on human history, and the violence that is carried out in its name, even in this world today. And they will say, "Yes, a New Message from God would be a very good thing right now."

But even they might have a great problem acknowledging the presence of the Messenger, to have a man in their midst who was actually sent into the world for this purpose. How would they relate to this person? If this person is who the New Message says he is, then they would have to honor him and respect him and receive him, or be amongst those who would once again deny the Revelation when it is given into the world.

It puts everyone on the spot. It challenges everyone. Oh, certainly, a new set of ideas and practices, yes, that might be very easy to accommodate. But to have a Messenger in your midst?

Well, for many people that would be a great enough challenge, such a great challenge that they will not even pay attention to the New Message from God. They will just be concerned with the Messenger, wanting to criticize or repudiate the Messenger. Or perhaps they will think the Messenger is like a postman—just delivering messages, a person of no significance, just a vehicle of transmission alone.

But God's Messengers have been some of the greatest people of all time in this world, and their demonstration and their personal teachings have been accorded the highest regard, even worshipped by many. So you cannot consider God's Messenger to be simply someone who delivers the mail or the post.

The Revelation itself is the biggest ever given to humanity and the most coherent because you are dealing now with a more educated world, a literate world, a world of global communication and global commerce, where a message can spread around the world, as the New Message from God is doing at this very moment.

It is not a Message for one tribe or one region. It is not God instructing one small group how to survive amidst adversity. It is not for one region of the world where one or two specific spiritual practices have been undertaken for a long time and this is simply a correction, a new understanding in light of a tradition, one tradition alone.

No, this is a Message for the whole world. It does not pay special homage to one people, one nation, one tribe or one group. No matter where you are from in the world or your social or economic standing, it speaks equally to you.

It is not here to rescue one people from oppression. It is not here to guide one group into a new land. It is not here to teach people how to transcend the world, but instead how to be in the world and serve the world, which is everyone's greater purpose ultimately in being here.

So then how do you regard the Messenger of such a monumental understanding, an understanding that not only brings wisdom of the ages from this one world, but brings Wisdom from the Greater Community of life in the universe? That has never been done before, for it was never needed before. But humanity now stands at the precipice of life in the universe and must prepare to engage in this— its greatest and most consequential challenge.

So the Messenger is not some unwitting person who is just chosen to bring information here to be consumed by consumers. It is a Revelation meant to change the course of human history, to give people a whole new understanding and way of looking at themselves, the world, and human destiny and the future of this world.

Certainly, the Messenger of such a Revelation must be someone extraordinary in the world, with an understanding far greater than what most people could ever honestly claim for themselves. In fact, because he is the vehicle of Revelation, he is unique in the whole world, for there is no one else who can bring the Revelation.

For God only sends one Revelation over the course of many years and centuries. It is sufficient, you see. If God sent many Revelations, there would be competing Revelations. People would be cast in opposition to each other. There would be great controversy, and the risk of corruption and collusion would be very great, you see.

So there is one Message and one Messenger. But people do not want to hear this because it means they must do something. They must face something. And ultimately they must change their lives, particularly if they want God to help them. For if you want God to help you, you really have to change your life.

So the Message and the Messenger then become agents of great change in the world, and for those who profit from the way things are at this moment, it will seem threatening and unsettling. And they will be disposed to try to rid themselves of it, or demean it at least, or destroy it if they can. For those who have a greater and more legitimate need in their life, they perhaps can see this as a redemption, as an empowerment, which it truly is.

How people respond to God speaking again to the world and sending a Messenger into the world is the great question and the great unknown. Even the Angelic Host does not know how this will turn out.

It is a test for the human heart in each person who can respond. It is a test of their integrity and self-honesty. Many people will think, "Well, God is just simply here to make my life work better for me. All I have to do is believe"—believe in an ideology or a religious teaching or the theory of a church or an institution. They think God is their servant, here to correct their errors, to improve their investments, to rescue them from the predicaments of life, and only then will they believe, as if God has to prove God to them. For they themselves cannot feel and know this on their own.

What you must understand here is that God's New Revelation is not simply a gift and a blessing upon the world, which it most certainly is. It is a test for humanity.

If humanity cannot respond, God will not punish the human family, but you will be left in a declining world facing opposition and intervention from the universe around you—unable to recognize the true nature of your predicament, unable to respond, unable to inspire people to cooperate together, which will be necessary to meet these two great challenges.

God does not punish. God simply withdraws. And that is a terrible enough thing in and of itself. You may pray to God for many things, of course—in times of real need, to meet difficulties, tragedies for yourself and your loved ones, and this is entirely understandable. And God will not retreat from this, for God never retreats from this.

But if the great Revelation for the world cannot be received sufficiently here, then what else is God going to do for you and for the world itself? You may still feel blessed by the Great Presence, but humanity itself will follow its path of decline and disintegration— blind, foolish, driven, only preoccupied with expediencies and short-term gain and profit. It knows not of its calamitous journey and refuses to recognize the obvious truth and error of its ways.

So the Messenger becomes important. In fact, he is the most important person in the world today. For without him and the Revelation, humanity is in grave peril. The world is being depleted. Humanity will run out of critical resources. Intervention is underway from certain predatory races who operate in secret in the world. How will you deal with these things? And who has the power and the commitment to deal with these things?

It is such a great challenge and difficulty that God has sent a New Revelation to the world to teach you how to live in a declining world, and to prepare you for a Greater Community of life, and to warn you of the Intervention that is occurring in the world and to empower people from all faiths, nations and tribes in gaining the strength of Knowledge that God has placed within each person, within each human heart.

Here there are no heroes to worship. Here there is no Judgment Day. Dispense with this foolishness.

You have a great and growing crisis in the world, greater than anything humanity as a whole has ever had to face before. God knows this and is sending the awareness, the warning, the blessing and the preparation. Get out of your self-preoccupation, and you can begin to see the bigger picture with greater clarity if you have the courage and the heart to do so.

People who will deny the Messenger are those who are afraid that their previous understanding might be challenged, that they may have to adjust and correct their thinking and change their approach to life. Here the rich will find it more difficult than the poor, for the poor are already in great need and do not have a great investment in the world.

Those who deny the Messenger will do so to protect their investments and their philosophy, their theology and their social position. They will expect that God will honor these things. But God has no regard for these things. Do you think the Lord of all the universes is concerned with the prestige of a handful of people in the world?

God is not even concerned with associating the New Revelation with predictions and prophecies from the past, for these are largely human inventions, or have become human inventions over the course of history as they have become altered and applied inappropriately. Prophecies are a message for a time—not for all time, not for all people, all places and all situations.

The people who will deny the Messenger are afraid of the Revelation. They are afraid they might have someone of this importance in their midst. They are afraid that they might have to challenge their own position in society. They are afraid to follow their own hearts. They will follow instead the fixations of their minds, their beliefs, their admonitions, their political associations—all the things that keep the individual in chains and unable to respond to the Presence of God within them.

Do you see what We are saying here? The Revelation casts a light upon all things, great and small, blessed and corrupt. It reveals corruption at every level, as if everyone who is hiding out gets revealed in the great Light of Revelation. Their position is shown to be what it truly is. Their weakness is exposed. Their compromise is revealed.

Only the truly honest and courageous are willing to face these things, recognizing the great need of their own soul to regain their connection to God and their greater purpose for being here.

Only those who realize the great danger facing human civilization will be able to overcome their anxiety and their considerations to be able to witness and investigate for themselves the meaning, the power and the grace of the Revelation.

This is the same problem that every great Messenger has had to face in coming into the world—great adversity, great dishonesty, great corruption, great misunderstanding, great misuse of religion, great misuse of political and economic power.

But now, you see, it is more formidable because now the whole world can react, not simply local officials. The New Revelation is going out to the whole world, so the resistance can come from the whole world—from every nation, every religion, every government, which in one way or another will feel challenged by this as the Message becomes ever more potent, and more and more people can recognize its efficacy and importance in the world.

So the Messenger can reach many more people in a very short period of time, which is necessary given the great crises on the horizon, but at the same time the resistance and the rejection can be overwhelming.

It took centuries for religions to gain recognition beyond their point of origin in the world, spread very slowly because communication was very slow. Travel and transportation were very slow. Now God's Revelation can be read by someone on the far side of the world with the click of a button.

Do you see the power of this? All people of good faith can be impacted once they become aware of the presence that God has spoken again. The power of this is tremendous because time is short. Humanity does not have decades or a century to figure out what to do in the face of its great challenges.

Humanity is running out of resources. It is running out of time. It must be very bold in how it faces things and resolves things, and not simply maintain what it has created from before.

Here there must be great strength, great courage, great honesty and great clarity in understanding what you are dealing with here. But even the most educated people are still handicapped by their own prejudices and lack of vision. Your universities do not teach Knowledge and wisdom really. They immerse people in information and perspectives. So you cannot look to the experts to see, to know and to act accordingly.

The gift is given to each person, and the Messenger will speak to this. You must find the power of Knowledge that God has placed within you. The Messenger will speak to this. You must bring balance and honesty into your relationships and affairs with others. The Messenger will speak to this.

You must prepare for a world in decline—not only practically on the outside, but even more importantly emotionally and psychologically on the inside, recognizing as you do so the power of guidance that God has given to you. The Messenger will speak of this.

The Messenger will speak of things so great and so imperative, not only for the world as a whole, but for you as an individual. This is not presented in anecdotes and pastoral stories. It is not presented enigmatically so that it has to be clarified by human commentary over the centuries. It is given simply, plainly, boldly and directly, and repeated very often so that the opportunity for recognition can be very great. Can people hear this and respond appropriately?

You must see that the Messenger is not simply someone carrying packages. Actually, part of the Revelation is within him. It is not revealed in the word or the writings. It is within him. He has the power of initiation in this sense.

But he is an older man now. He has had to endure a very long preparation and many difficulties along the way. There is very little time to receive him, and anyone who does so will be blessed in the interchange, whether they can recognize it in the moment or not.

Here you must deal with both the Messenger and the Revelation itself. You cannot have one without the other, for they are complete, you see. To not recognize the Messenger is to misunderstand the process of Revelation, the meaning of its presence in the world, the understanding it reveals about how God works in the world and how God serves whole worlds in a universe full of intelligent life.

Likewise, you cannot make a hero and a god out of the Messenger. Though he does deserve great respect and accord, he is not a god. But none of the Messengers have been gods. They are just the most important people in the world, that is all. They are not perfect. They do not have colossal powers, but they are a demonstration of Revelation. They are human. You can see their fallibilities if you really look for it. It is what they bring into the world—the fact that they are a vehicle for something greater, a vessel for something greater—that makes their power and presence so important in the world whenever they appear.

They do not appear very often, you see, for while every age has its prophets, and often more than one, only once in a millennium is a New Revelation from God brought into the world. And it is only brought into the world at a time of great change, great opportunity and great hazard.

If you can understand what We are saying to you today, you will see that you are living at a time of Revelation—a very, very important time to be in the world, a very significant turning point for the world.

If you can see this, you will think of your life differently, rather than just as a person struggling to have things and to get along with others and to stay healthy, safe and secure. You will see that your life, really, here has a greater dimension and a greater purpose, and that this purpose in some way, directly or indirectly, is related to living at a time of Revelation.

It is like you are living at a moment in history that only comes once every one or two thousand years. That makes your presence in the world especially important, so much so that people in the future will look back with envy upon those who lived at this time. And they will say, "Did they recognize the Revelation? Did they recognize the Messenger?"

You are blessed to be here in the world at this time, to be able to hear Our words, my goodness. You have no idea how blessed you are, or what it could mean for your life and for others who know you, or could hear you speak to them.

From Heaven's standpoint, this is a great and significant blessing and opportunity. But what Heaven knows is different from what people want. And what people think is very different from what Heaven considers to be true and important.

The Messenger will be resisted and demeaned, but he must have representatives. He must have witnesses. Or the world will crush him and try to cancel out his presence and his gift to the world.

That is why We say everyone who knows of the Messenger is challenged to respond. It is not enough to say, "Well, this person claims to have a New Message from God, but I don't know." That is not honest. Within your heart, you can know, and you are meant to know.

People think, "Oh, messengers come all the time. There are always messengers in the world." And they say this because they do not want to face the fact that something of great significance is happening in the world today. And they do not really want to deal with it. Or perhaps they are jealous that they are not the messenger. Or they think everyone is a messenger, or messengers are as common as anything, they are all over the place, delivering messages.

These people do not want to deal with the reality of the situation. They do not want to be called to attention by it. They do not want to be impacted. They do not want to have to respond. They do not want to have to deal with the challenge and the great opportunity that Revelation brings to them. They simply want to keep doing what they are doing and not be troubled by these things.

This all, of course, is a problem of lack of self-honesty and honesty with others—a great difficulty in the human family, and a great difficulty throughout the universe, We might say.

You must see that the Messenger is no ordinary person. Without trying to deify him or elevate him to some lofty, perfect position, you must recognize that he is carrying the Revelation. Through hardship, through illness, through opposition, he is carrying it. And if you can receive and respond to it, you must help him in some way because he cannot alone bring this forth. He will need many witnesses and many advocates.

It is a strange thing that people pray for redemption. They pray to have a new life. They pray to be freed from the misery, the shame, the guilt and the regrets from their past. And so when the gift comes to them, they do not want to deal with it. When the answer for them comes, well, it is too big. It is too difficult. It is too uncomfortable. It is socially unacceptable. They are perhaps incensed that it is brought by only one person, and there can only be one person. It runs against their egalitarian views, perhaps, their democratic notions because they think they know how Revelation occurs or should occur. The Messenger will have to face, and is facing today, all of these things.

Then the Messenger has to face the people who want to be a part of all this, but they want to be served and saved and nourished. They bring their problems, their weakness, their disabilities, expecting the Message and the Messenger to resolve all things for them when, in fact, they have to work upon these things themselves. And the Revelation gives them the pathway to do this.

Instead of coming to serve the Revelation, they only want to be served by it. Perhaps, in the beginning, their need is great and the Revelation will serve them, but everyone is sent into the world to be contributors. And once they gain the health and the freedom to do this, that is their task. That is their calling, you see. There is no personal fulfillment aside from this. It is because of your deeper nature, because of where you have come from and what you will return to, that this is truly the case.

The Messenger will speak of these things. He is not here to break things down. He is not here to destroy the institutions. He is not here to speak out harshly against human institutions, governments and religious authorities.

He is here to bring Grace and the great Love of God and the requirement that people respond to their deeper nature and take the Steps to Knowledge, the deeper intelligence that God has placed within them to guide them.

He brings then blessings, empowerment and requirements. The Wisdom he brings is greater than what any person could ever understand, greater even than the Messenger understands. That is why no one else can claim to do this. It would be false to make such a claim.

This is the challenge before you, you see, you who are hearing Our words. It is not about belief, for that is of the mind. This is about the soul and your heart and your deeper nature, not the fixations of the mind.

To reject the Revelation because it does not conform to your beliefs is utterly foolish and arrogant because Revelation is always here to take you beyond your current understanding, to reveal to you things you have not seen or could not see on your own.

So to reject the Revelation because it does not fit your definitions or your religious ideas is simply to turn your back on that which could lift you up and restore and redeem your life. The Messenger will speak of these things.

Do you see the challenge here? You cannot make a deal with God. And you cannot come to God on your own terms. God sets the terms and the requirements and provides the opportunities, given here in a pure form—without human corruption; without the misuse of others; without being maligned and misused by institutions, governments and so forth. It is here in a pure form.

God has spoken again, and it is here. It is pure. But you must find that place within you that is pure to respond to it honestly and responsibly.

Then you can look at the Messenger with gratitude and be grateful for his presence and for those who sent him into the world. Be grateful for your presence and what his presence could mean for your life— the resolution, the clarity, the grace and the opportunity this brings to you and to others through you.

Many people will say they pray for redemption and restoration for themselves, their loved ones and for the whole world, but they do not want it to come today because today would be too inconvenient. But it is here today. And it is inconvenient. And it is challenging. And it is wonderful.

It shows you what is strong within you and what is weak, what must lead and what must follow. It restores to you your integrity, your dignity and your greater purpose in the world because it is a gift from God and not a human invention.

Honor the Messenger and help him in any way you can. And accept that you must prepare for your greater role. You are not ready at this moment. And be grateful that the preparation has been given, and that the wisdom of the world can help you in this, and that the corruption and tragedy of the world can show you the great need for this.

Be grateful, for in gratitude you will know your own heart. And you will remember those who sent you here, so very long ago.

CHAPTER 8

FACING THE LIGHT OF REVELATION

As revealed to
Marshall Vian Summers
on August 18, 2012
in Boulder, Colorado

People do not realize what the Messenger is facing in the world. For him, it is a very difficult thing, and he is reluctant to accept it because it is so very difficult—with so much risk and uncertainty and the assurance of rejection and denial. It is a very difficult thing, you see.

For the Messengers, this has always been the case. And while they have been the most important people in all of human history, they have also had some of the most difficult tasks—tasks which they themselves would never choose for themselves, but which were given to them, with great emphasis.

In fact, the miracle of their work is the miracle of their acceptance and their willingness to follow a pattern and a pathway not of their own making or their own design, to venture forth without a grand scheme or plan—without knowing all the steps and what they would require and what must be developed within them, what must be released and what it would require of those who were called to assist them and follow them.

So while they had the biggest task in the world, they also had the least information to begin with. Only the certainty that it must be done. Only the power of the engagement with the Angelic Assembly. Only the conviction deep within them that this is it. This is everything they have prepared for. This is everything that they must do.

There is no alternative. There is no other life to choose. There is no way out. You cannot excuse yourself, you see, when you reach this point. You must get on that ship sailing to the New World, with all the hazards that that involves and the uncertainty of what you will find and experience when you arrive.

For the Messenger, the hazard is both failure and success. If he fails to reach enough people in the world, then his Message may not take hold here, may fall into obscurity and be altered and changed by people for their own purposes and desires.

But, in a way, success holds greater difficulty for the Messenger, for with success comes recognition, and with recognition comes misfortune. With recognition comes acceptance that is not true—people rushing to meet the Messenger, but for all the wrong reasons, wanting special favors, wanting miracles, wanting special dispensations, wanting to be with the Messenger, to be part of his special entourage, to travel with him and be his companion and to claim all of the significance and recognition for this.

Then there will be people who will think the Messenger is their mate and their partner. Then there will be people who will come, but who are really not willing to put in the effort and the self-examination and the work that are required to rise to this great occasion, certainly the greatest occasion of this time in the world.

Yes, they have come for the right reasons, but they do not know themselves enough to see where they could fail, to see where they are weak and vulnerable, to see where they could fall under persuasion from other forces and step back into the shadows once the road becomes more difficult and challenging.

Some will fade away. They cannot accept the challenge. They cannot face the honesty that this will require within themselves even though they are called to this situation, even though it is the right place and time for them.

Amongst those who will reject the Messenger are all those who are protecting their position, their investment, their ideology, their arrogance, their significance, their pride, their position in society, their position in academia, their position in the theological community.

There are those who will reject the Messenger because he does not bring them gifts and miracles and relieve them from all of their difficulties—promising ecstasy, bliss and paradise in the future. They have to be sold on the truth. They cannot see it clearly themselves. They will want the Messenger to prove himself to them, when in reality they must prove themselves to him.

Then there are all the false messengers who, out of pride and arrogance and insecurity, will proclaim they have a new message from God or something equivalent to that. And they may be very persuasive, very aggressive, very charming, charismatic. But their message has no substance. It is not original in any sense. While it may make some different intellectual associations, it is not a New Revelation. It does not bring a new reality into the world. It does not prepare humanity for the future. It does not encompass all of life in this world and beyond. It is the product of their imagination, curiosity and reckless association.

And they will fail the test, you see, and therefore the Messenger will be associated with them—the false messenger. "Oh, we have had so many false messengers before. We have been warned of the false messengers." Therefore, the real Messenger will be associated with them.

People want the Messenger to fit their expectations and definitions, you see. They want him to be pure, magnanimous, magnificent, all powerful, able to do things that no one else can do to prove himself to them, when in reality they must prove themselves to him.

The previous Messengers have been so exalted and embellished and amplified that they have become like gods, if not called gods directly. Therefore, [people think] a new Messenger must have all the qualities that have been added on and associated with the previous great Messengers in the world. So the expectations are unrealistic and have nothing to do with the real qualities of the Messenger or what qualifies this individual to make this proclamation and to assume this greater role in the world.

People think there are no future Messengers. "The Prophet was the last Messenger. The Christ was the last Messenger. There need be no others." But this is to say that God has nothing else to say to humanity, that God has lost interest in humanity and will not prepare humanity for the greatest events in human history, which it is now beginning to face: a declining world, a diminishing world, a world of declining resources, violent weather and ever-growing economic and political instability; a world facing global crises now, not simply regional or local ones; a world facing intervention from the universe around you by small invasive groups who are here to take advantage of human weakness and expectations.

None of God's previous Revelations can prepare you for this. None of God's previous Revelations were given to speak to all of humanity at the very outset. For God's New Message is not for one group or one region or one tribe. It is a Message to the whole world, right now, for everyone is facing the Great Waves of change coming to the world, and everyone is facing a universe full of intelligent life, a non-human universe of which humanity knows nothing at all.

Would God let humanity fail collectively and completely in the face of either or both of these great thresholds, while people are fighting and killing each other over who the Prophet should be or what the truth should be or what their definition of God should be, with all of the enmity, cruelty, misery and unforgiveness in the past to bolster and fortify these attitudes and beliefs?

Without a New Revelation, humanity will break down into crisis after crisis after crisis as food, water and energy become more scarce and difficult to find—leading to wars of desperation, leading to violence on a scale never seen in the world before.

People cannot see this, not because it is not apparent, not because its signs are not being demonstrated in the world, but because they do not have the strength or the courage or the faith to face things of this magnitude. They will think it is the end times: the end of the world has finally come. But it is the beginning of a great transition.

And the outcome of that transition will be determined in the next twenty to thirty years—whether humanity will be a deprived and subjugated race, subjugated by foreign races who have planted themselves here under the disguise of offering hope and redemption to a struggling humanity. Or will humanity rise up and become a strong and independent race in the universe, establishing its own boundaries and rules of engagement with life beyond? Will humanity learn to live in a world of diminishing resources, a world requiring greater equanimity, cooperation, forgiveness and contribution?

Only God knows. People are lost in the past. They are moving forward looking behind themselves. They do not see what is coming over the horizon. They do not see because they are too afraid, too obsessed, too preoccupied and too full of their own ideas and beliefs, too arrogant, too ignorant. While life is giving them the signs and the warnings, they do not see. They do not hear. They do not respond.

So God must send a New Revelation into the world and send a new Messenger into the world to prepare humanity for these greatest of all events. And he will have to face all that the previous Messengers had to face. But he will have to face even more, for now he is speaking to the whole world—people from many countries all at once, people from many cultures and many religions all at once. The adversity he will face could surely be greater than anything a previous Messenger had to face in their time, in their circumstances.

The resistance to God's Revelation will come from many quarters—governments, religious institutions, other people competing for pre-eminence. It will be dismissed by secularists and scientists, thinking that, "Well, this is another foolishness, thinking that God is speaking again." Because they have made their ideals and their science their religion, and like all other religious figures who are not open to Revelation, they will dismiss it for the very same reasons.

So the Messenger has the great opportunity to speak to the world in broadcast and in the written word, at once reaching a world not in centuries but in decades. But the adversity he will have to encounter could be very significant.

And he will have to be protected by those who love him. And he will have to be assisted by those who are called to him. And they will have to realize that they cannot fail. They cannot fall away or fade into the shadows. They must be strong. They must be honest. They must be willing to travel a path that challenges them, uplifts them and requires great things from them, for this is how people are redeemed, you see.

God does not wave a wand and make all of your disabilities, frustrations and conflicts disappear. God gives you great things to do, important things to do, things that you can do, things that are needed. And it is through this, if you can find and follow this greater counsel, that your redemption will be underway.

The separated are reclaimed through Knowledge, the deeper intelligence that is placed within all sentient life. They are saved through following Knowledge, which leads to a life of service and contribution.

God's New Revelation speaks of these things in great detail, answering many questions concerning them. For God's Revelation, given through the Angelic Assembly, is the most expansive ever given—given now to a world that is far more educated, a world of global communications, a world of global commerce, a world facing global problems and potential calamities.

God is giving now a Message, not in parables, not in stories, not in [anecdotes], but in the clearest possible words that can be translated easily and clearly into other languages, given with much repetition, given with much clarification, given with its own commentary so it does not rely upon future human commentary to define what it means for people.

God's New Revelation is to bring you close to God and what God wants you to do, and what you are here to do, and to show you how to follow what you are here to do and to discern it from all the other voices and forces and influences in your mind.

God has given you the Steps to Knowledge to take on the pathway so that you may learn to connect your worldly mind in service to the greater mind within you in such a way that all of your skills are enhanced and all of your disabilities are reduced.

Only God could do this for every person. You cannot possibly understand this. You will bring every argument against it, but your arguments only prove you cannot understand how God works through people or what God intends to do.

For God's Word now is not merely for this moment, for the crisis of this day, but for the crisis of 25 years from now and 50 years from now and 100 years from now. And that is why God has given you the Revelation about Life in the Universe, so that you can prepare for this reality. Never has anything like this ever been given to humanity before.

To face this, to receive this, to allow this to begin the process of redemption in your life, you must be willing to evaluate your life, to change your life where it is necessary, to be courageous in this regard, to be determined in this regard, to give up your other gods—your god of obligations, your god of infatuation, your god of accumulation— your other gods. Not to make you a renunciate, but to make you a person capable and free enough to undertake a greater work and service in the world.

Only God knows what this means. For you cannot serve the world if you are angry with the world. You cannot serve people if you do not love them. You cannot even face your enemies if you condemn them completely. God knows what this means.

For the first time in history, you are able to see now the process of Revelation and to receive it in a pure form, without it being altered or reconstructed later by those who did not know the Messenger.

This is the greatest moment, you see, that through the wonders of technology, you can hear the Voice of Revelation: a Voice like that that spoke to the Jesus, the Buddha and the Muhammad and the other great Emissaries, who remain unrecognized in the world.

The challenge is upon you, then, for the Messenger is not here to prove himself to you. You must prove yourself to him and to those who sent him. Deny him, and you deny those who sent him. You deny the Lord of the universe to protect your religious ideas, your social ideas, your political ideas, your grievances, your fears, your condemnation of religion, your pride, your arrogance, your ignorance, your stupidity without even looking to see what the Revelation really is.

You will see experts doing this—well-educated people, theologians, philosophers, people you admire—acting so foolishly, so blindly. For Knowledge is not strong enough within them to call them to see the New Message and to consider it seriously.

They will reject it on philosophical grounds. They will say, "Well, we don't think of God like this anymore." They do not know what they are talking about. They think they know how God works, what God is, how God manifests, how God influences, how God brings about correction? No, they have the God of antiquity as their reference point, or perhaps some recent philosophy. They cannot see this clearly because they cannot approach it clearly. They will think it is something else.

The Messenger will have to face all of this, you see. And so disheartening it will be for him. He is a humble man. He has been sent into the world for this purpose. He takes it into the world reluctantly, knowing the great hazards, dangers and disappointments. Even people he might admire will turn against him. Even those who think they know him—his family members, perhaps—will turn against him. For who knows a Messenger from God at the time of Revelation?

When you recognize he has the most difficult task in the world and the greatest Message for the world, you will want to help him. And you will have to look and see in your own heart what you are willing to do [in order] to do this given your circumstances, your health and your true abilities. The challenge is upon the recipient at a time of Revelation, you see.

The Messenger brings the Message. He does not have to do circus tricks for people. He does not have to please them and appease them and give them what they want and meet their expectations and fulfill their ambitions, for he will not do these things.

Messengers before were demonized and destroyed because they did not give people what they wanted. They could not be used as a resource by those who heard them and saw them and received them.

You will see this again. People try to profit off the situation like they try to profit off of every situation, as if they were locusts upon the land. But you cannot profit from the Messenger unless you can receive the Revelation and take the Steps to Knowledge yourself.

And do not take the position that you do not know because that is not really honest, you see. "Well, I don't know about this Messenger. I just don't know." That is not really honest. You are not taking this deeply enough. For in your heart, you can see and know this. Do not hide [behind] indecision.

The challenge is upon the recipient at a time of Revelation. And the Messenger will see before him, and you will see if you travel with him, all manner of self-deception, self-denial, confabulation, all manner of foolishness, all manner of greed, all manner of ambition placed before him in the Light of Revelation. For everything that is impure, everything that is corrupt, everything that is misguided will be revealed in the Light of Revelation because it is pure. And it will reveal the impurity of everything around it.

That is why people run the other way. That is why people do not want to look. That is why people put up walls and cast stones. They do not want to have their impurities revealed to them. They do not want to have to reconsider their core beliefs. They do not want to have to rethink their religion in light of the New Revelation. They do not want to have to face themselves and the life that they have led, and how compromised it has really been and dishonest in so many ways. But that is what happens at a time of Revelation.

In the past, people made the Messenger a god, unlike them. "Oh, we never have to be like him, so therefore we are off the hook. We are relieved from the challenge of Revelation." They made the Messenger so lofty and special, his position so unattainable, that they would never have to really work very hard, you see.

The Messenger will have to face all of this. You cannot imagine the discouragement. You cannot imagine the difficulty. You cannot imagine the tragedy of human failure that will be revealed in the Light of Revelation.

But the Revelation brings power, strength, integrity and dignity to the person and asks them to do what they know they must do, and to be honest enough to see this and to follow this, without trying to compromise or make some kind of deal.

The New Message brings blessing upon all peoples, from all faith traditions, from all nations, from all economic classes of people—the rich, the poor, everyone in between. It brings the blessing of an inner revelation with Knowledge. It brings preparation for a world that everyone will have to face together. It brings the Revelation about the universe that everyone will have to face together. It brings the mystery of one's inner life—the power and the presence of Knowledge that exists beyond the realm and the reach of the intellect.

You cannot even imagine what this can do for the individual. Even if they take little steps, it will begin to strengthen them and give them courage they did not have before.

God blesses the separated, the lonely and the miserable—whether they be rich or poor. And the Revelation is for them, and for you and for everyone in the world who can receive it. For many must receive this Revelation for it to have its great impact on human awareness, human cooperation, the cessation of war and the preparation for the Greater Community that must begin.

Do not make the Messenger your controversy. Make your own response to the Message the controversy. Your controversy is your indecision about whether you will be a real and honest person, and your investment in those things that take you away from this and what it has cost you and what you are going to do about it. That is the controversy. The controversy is not the theological excellence of the New Revelation, according to what is considered to be true thus far in the human realm, as if humanity could really understand these things.

The real controversy is how people will respond at a time of Revelation—whether they will become obsessed with the Messenger and their expectations and demands of him, or whether they will take to heart what the Revelation is really giving to them and communicating to them, over and over again.

People have been praying honestly, earnestly, for redemption, for deliverance, to improve their circumstances and the quality of their lives, to improve their health and the health of those they love, to improve their environment, to improve their world. And God has finally answered in a Message for everyone—not just a little message for one tribe or group, but a Message for the whole world because the whole world needs this Message now.

Here you do not leave your faith, your religious tradition. You simply bring the Revelation into it—to amplify it; to make it greater, more potent, more powerful; infuse it with the Spirit, the intent and the great Love of God.

That which has become old, dried up, irrelevant, lacking passion, meaning, purpose and application now is infused with everything that will make it alive.

For even the Christians must become people willing to face the Great Waves of change and humanity's emergence into a Greater Community of life. The Muslims, the Jews, the Buddhists—all the religious groups, large and small—are all facing the same challenges and the risk of calamity. They all need a New Revelation from God.

They all need to hear the Messenger—honestly, patiently considering everything he brings.

This is the time of Revelation. There is a Messenger in the world. He brings a Revelation unlike anything that has been given before, speaking of greater things that were never considered or needed before. He brings the clarification of spirituality at the level of Knowledge. He speaks of that which has always been true, and of that which has never been considered.

Hear him. Receive him. Be honest. You do not know who he is or what he brings yet until you give this your honest, objective consideration—being willing to be challenged, being willing to reconsider your ideas, being willing to think again where you stand and what is real and what is happening in your life and the world around you.

God and the Angelic Presence watch over the world to see how people will respond, who will respond, how will they respond, the purity of their response, their willingness to undergo deep transformation within themselves in light of the Revelation. Who will object, who will resist, who will fight against this, who will try to destroy the New Message from God and God's Messenger in the world?

The eyes of Heaven will be watching. The test is for humanity. For this is not only a great gift, the greatest you can imagine, it is also a test. For learning is always a test, and a great learning is a great test. And a great need is a great test. And living in physical reality is a great test. The eyes of Heaven will be watching to see how and if their Messenger is received here. Let this be your understanding.

CHAPTER 9

THE JOURNEY OF THE MESSENGER

As revealed to
Marshall Vian Summers
on July 14, 2013
in Boulder, Colorado

God has sent the Messenger into the world at a time of great change and increasing uncertainty. He is the one Messenger for the world though it will be difficult for many people to accept this, given their previous notions and investments.

He has prepared long for this. He has come from the Angelic Assembly, of which he is a part. In the world, he is a man. He is imperfect, but all the great Messengers have been imperfect.

He is the one because he was sent into the world for this purpose, and he comes from the Assembly. What he will provide no individual could provide, no matter how inspired or how educated they might be, for they cannot bring the Will and the Power of Heaven through their words and proclamation.

But the true Messenger not only brings the Will and Power of Heaven, but the Voice of Heaven itself—the Voice of the Assembly speaking as one, the many speaking as one—a reality you cannot consider with your intellect. It is far too limited for this.

There will be those who can recognize the Messenger immediately, but for most others it will have to be learned through time and demonstration, for they have much to clear in their own minds before they can see something of this magnitude. They will want proof in various forms. And some of their expectations will be met and others will not, for God is not bound by these things.

The Messengers of antiquity, their lives have been so altered and construed over the ages that nobody really knows who they were now in a real and practical sense. But in truth no one can understand the life of the Messenger. For the Messengers come from the Angelic Assembly. They are not the sons and daughters of God, for God does not have sons and daughters. That is merely a worldly understanding. It does not apply to Creation.

So the Messenger is in the world. He has been prepared for so very long. It has taken a great deal of time to receive a Revelation more expansive and inclusive than anything that has ever been given to this world, given now plainly and clearly, in a world of global communications and global commerce, no longer clothed in anecdotes or pastoral themes or poetic images, but spoken clearly with much repetition so that it can be heard over time; given now using the technology of this era, which was never available before; given now to speak to the whole world at once, not just one tribe or group or region—a Message so great because it represents the God of the universe and what God is doing in the entire universe, which has never been revealed before. For humanity was not educated or developed enough to consider such great things, save but a few individuals.

You do not yet realize the perfection of this and why it must be so. For what God is doing in the world can only be known, if you understand what God is doing in the universe as a whole. And such a Revelation has never been given until now. It is with the Messenger. It is given in the Revelation.

The future of this world and the great challenge facing the human family are revealed in the Revelation.

The meaning of each person's spirituality and what unites people everywhere are contained in the Revelation.

The meaning and purpose of all the religious traditions, which seem so different in contrast to one another, are given in the Revelation.

The meaning of true relationship, true love, true commitment, true devotion is given in the Revelation.

Only someone from the Angelic Assembly could bring something of this magnitude into the world, presented in a form never seen before—wedding ancient wisdom with realizations and truth that have never been clearly understood, save but by a very, very few.

But it is the whole world now that must receive this, to prepare for the great change that is coming for the world and to prepare for humanity's encounter with a universe of intelligent life, a non-human universe where freedom is rare. It is the greatest challenge humanity has ever faced and will have the greatest consequences for your life and for the future of every person, both now and into the future.

The Messenger carries this like a fire. It has been presented so purely that you can hear the Voice of Revelation, which was never possible before for obvious reasons. Pure, uncorrupted, undefiled, unwedded to other ideas, beliefs or traditions, it is pure. But to recognize this and to receive it, your mind must be pure or pure enough so that you can see, so that you can hear, so that you can understand.

Without this, you are trapped by your judgments, your condemnation, your opinions and all that you have invested yourself in, which now stand in the way of the greatest event of your time, happening in your midst, during the time of the Messenger.

He walks as a humble man, but people do not see. They do not recognize him. He speaks with clarity and sincerity and humility, but people do not hear. They cannot respond.

But this is the challenge that has faced all of the Messengers in all eras. It is the outcome of living in Separation in a world that has been so darkened by human violence and ignorance and tragedy that people do not know how to see. They do not know how to hear. They do not know how to know. They have lost their connection with the deeper Knowledge that God has placed within them—that is here to guide them, to protect them and to prepare them for a greater life of service in the world.

So the Messenger walks and speaks, but very few can hear at first. And to hear the Messenger, you must really listen, not trying to compare what he says with what you think already, but with a desire to see beyond your current notions and confusion. He brings the light of clarity, but if you are living in the fog of confusion, you will not see this light. It will be in your midst, but you will only see other things.

How then will this Messenger—an individual who comes into the world, oh, only perhaps one in a millennium—how will he speak to a whole world and speak to them in such a way that his Message will find enough response to prepare humanity for the great change that is coming and that is upon them already? For the hour is late, and people are still living in a dream or a nightmare, depending upon their circumstances.

How will he speak to a whole world at once? It will not occur from him preaching from a street corner or talking to small groups alone. He must broadcast the Message using the technology and the freedom that he has to do this. In the future, this freedom may not exist, so this is the great window of opportunity and necessity for the world.

It will be a great challenge for many to hear the Revelation. It will challenge their ideas, their assumptions, their grievances, their attitudes and most certainly the compromises they have made in their own lives, which have placed them in such jeopardy and misery and unhappiness. Yet better to escape the darkness than to try to think it is filled with light.

The Messenger will broadcast into the world, and he will continue to do this, for it is far too unsafe for him to speak in public very often. He will be interviewed infrequently, but the interviewers will likely not understand. For he must proclaim that which is essential, that which speaks beyond the interests of one person alone, to the greater need of the human heart and soul and to the greater need for humanity to prepare for a world that will be so very different, that it is changing at a phenomenal pace, even at this very moment.

He will bring Wisdom and Knowledge from the universe. He will open the doors to life in the universe. He will speak of the Great Waves of change coming to the world. He will speak of relationships and higher purpose. He will speak of the power of Knowledge, the great intelligence that lives within each person, waiting to be discovered.

He will speak of the journey of the soul. He will speak of that which is true in every religion. And he will speak out against much that is false in every religion because he brings great correction with him. For this correction must be given, or the Revelation will not be understood. For when God speaks, it is always in great contrast to what humanity has collectively assumed to be true and to the many errors in its thinking and assumptions and understanding of the past.

God brings to the part of Creation living in Separation the great promise of redemption without the threat of Hell and damnation, for God does not send any part of Creation into damnation.

But the Message must be pure. It must be clear. It cannot be a compromise. It cannot be designed merely to appeal to people's current notions and appetites. It must bring great warning, power and restoration. For such great Revelations only happen at pivotal times of humanity's history and evolution.

You are fortunate to be living at a time of Revelation. It is the greatest time ever to be in the world. And you are here. You have been sent here to be living at this time—a time of great tribulation and upheaval, a time of great difficulty—living in a world of diminishing resources and growing population.

What will give you the strength and the power to avoid constant war and constant strife? Even the religions have taken up arms, once again. In a world full of combatants striving for who will have access to what is left, how will cooperation, how will justice, how will provision be established in a world under these conditions?

People have ideas, of course, but only God knows what will really be true and what will really be efficacious and fruitful in time.

God loves the world and will not see humanity destroy human civilization out of ignorance, fear and greed. So much has been invested in this world. It is an important world in a universe filled with countless races, countless religions. Only God knows.

To stand against this, to deny this, is the epitome of arrogance and ignorance and presumption. To think that God cannot send a new Messenger into the world is pure folly and arrogance. For not even God's Messengers will know what God will do next. Not even the scriptures can say what God will do next. Not even the Angelic Presence and Assembly can say what God will do next.

The Messenger will broadcast to the world, and he will make the Revelation as available as he can. And he will require tremendous support and assistance to do this. And his life will be imperiled from many different forces as he undertakes this great mission.

And he will have to find those who have the eyes to see and the ears to hear, who have been sent into the world to assist him. But they will have to follow him. They will have to receive. And they will have to give.

One man cannot do this alone. Even if he is anointed amongst the Angelic, he cannot do this alone. He will need great assistance and support.

And in your heart, you will know if that is your calling. But to know your heart, you must dip beneath the surface of your mind and escape from the ravage of your own ideas, the confusion of your mind, into a deeper realm within yourself where greater things can be seen and known.

And to make this possible, the Creator of all life has provided the Steps to Knowledge, a roadmap into the part of you that is permanent and true, powerful and fearless, gracious, but strong and determined—a part of you you barely know or have never known, but which resides at the foundation of your Being.

The purpose of all religion is to bring you to this. But the purpose of all religion has been lost and overlaid with human adoption, human institutions, human ideology, human power and dominance. It would take a great teacher in any tradition to find the true path to Knowledge there.

And there is no time for this now, for humanity must have the opportunity to prepare for the universe—a Greater Community of life. It must have the opportunity, the wisdom and the need to prepare for a world undergoing convulsive change.

Enough people must see and know this for the Revelation to take hold and for its power to be felt and expressed sufficiently in the world to overcome the fear, hatred, anger and anguish that dominate so many people's minds and that determine so many outcomes around the world.

The Messenger is an older man. His years are precious. He has been through great difficulty—adversity, illness, opposition. It has required remarkable patience and forbearance, humility and sacrifice for him to bring this into the world.

Now he will broadcast and present. And a few will be assigned to teach—assigned by him and the Assembly so that people understand his declaration, so that people understand who he is, why he is here and what he has brought to humanity—that which humanity cannot give itself.

It is the great blessing upon the world. It is the great hope for humanity. It promises the restoration of the religious traditions and provides the foundation for their unity together. It is a counterpoint to all that has been done to corrupt them. It is God's response and God's direction, God's Power and God's Presence, you see.

To come to the Messenger, you must first come to the Revelation, for the teaching is more important than the teacher. The Message is more important than the Messenger in time. The Messenger will pass from this world, but the Message will remain. Whether it will become corrupted and alloyed with other things will be determined by the purity of his followers and those who can respond to a New Message from God.

The Messenger will give teachings and clarification, but he will not be available to everyone, for his time is precious. His journey is great. His mission is tremendous.

Heaven watches to see who can respond. Heaven watches to see who will receive him as the Messenger. Heaven watches to see those who will deny him, ridicule him or condemn him.

It is a great trial for humanity. It is a great test. Can humanity receive a New Message from God—given not to one tribe or one region or one group, but to a whole world and received in time to prepare humanity for the great change that is coming to the world?

Time is of the essence now. You do not have a century to consider these things. This is not a plaything for the idle or the indolent. This is not merely a philosophy for philosophers to discuss and to debate. This is not a form of entertainment for those who have no seriousness about their life and no value for themselves.

You can hear the Messenger. You can see the Messenger. You can receive the Revelation given now in the purest form imaginable.

It is your challenge. It is your opportunity. It will bring to you that which lives within you, which is great. It will show you the way out of the jungle of confusion. It will give you the strength that God has given you and the responsibility that you proclaimed before coming into this world. It will return to you your strength, your dignity, your power and your purpose. Can you receive these things?

The blessing is here. God has spoken again. The Messenger has been sent into the world. He brings with him a Message of tremendous scope, power and inclusion. He has given his life for this. It is a great calling to assist and support him. It will make all the difference for humanity, the great difference in the times to come.

CHAPTER 10

THE PROPHET

As revealed to
Marshall Vian Summers
on July 23, 2009
in Damascus, Syria

Every millennium a New Messenger is sent into the world to prepare humanity for the next stage of its development and to warn humanity of the great dangers that have not arisen before, to prepare humanity for what it must face and what it must overcome, both now and into the future.

God's Revelations are rare and are long lasting. They are sent here to give to humanity what it could not give itself, and to rekindle the spiritual fire that has grown cold in the world, to revitalize the religious spirit, which has become so dormant under the weight and the oppression of religious belief and edicts.

Humanity is now facing its greatest challenges, greater than anything it has ever had to face before. It is facing a world in decline—a world of declining resources, a world whose environment has been so seriously abused and disrupted that there will have to be a different adaptation for humanity to survive in the world into the future. And humanity is facing intervention from races in the universe who are here to take advantage of a weak and divided humanity. Never before has the human family as a whole been so challenged.

You have reached this great threshold because of human behavior and because of the evolution of the human race itself. For sooner or later you would draw attention from the universe around you and intervention would follow. Sooner or later you would deplete your natural inheritance in the world to such a degree that the world would begin to change on its own in ways that would not be beneficial to humanity's ability to live here. Eventually, humanity would have to enter a more mature phase of its evolution, outgrowing its recklessness, its violence, its conflicts and its stupidity.

It is into this environment now that the Messenger is sent, a Prophet for this time and for this age—an age that will see a tremendous upheaval and disruption, an age where humanity will have to adapt to a changing planet and have to face the reality that it exists and always has existed in a Greater Community of intelligent life in the universe.

There is no escaping this reality. Running away into fantasy or denial, hiding behind human reason and preference only further humanity's vulnerability and make it more difficult for you to recognize and to adapt to a changing world.

It is into this situation that the Messenger is sent, and his prophecy will be the prophecy from the Creator—a great warning for humanity, a great blessing for humanity, a great preparation for the future, a preparation that humanity could not provide for itself.

In this sense, then, humanity is being rescued. But will the gift be recognized? Will the Messenger be recognized? Will the warning be heeded? And will the blessing be received?

Many people feel that God has finished speaking to the human family, that there will be no further Revelations, that a Messenger will no longer be sent into the world, as if God has nothing else to say to humanity as it faces its greatest tribulations.

But this is blind, and this is foolish. It is arrogant to assume what God will or will not do. You cannot hide behind the scriptures. You cannot hide behind science or rationality. You cannot look backwards, for you must look forward now to see what is coming over the horizon and to see that you are in a time of Revelation.

The Messenger has been sent. He is in the world today. He is not a superman. He is not going to perform miracles for the masses. He is not like a carnival act to impress people. His gift is deeper and richer, more profound and long lasting. He is not a sensation. He has the gift that no other person in the world has. He is the Prophet for this age.

If you cannot receive this, then you are holding onto your previous beliefs and assumptions, driven by fear that you may have to face something entirely new—a new world, a new life, a New Revelation.

In the past, whenever God has provided a Revelation for the world, it was resisted and denied and denounced for the very same reasons, from the very same state of mind that the New Message from God will be denounced and reviled and distrusted.

It is the problem of human denial, of course. It is the problem of people living in the past, unable to respond to the present and to the future with any degree of clarity or wisdom.

The future is upon you. The world will be unrecognizable in twenty years. You have nowhere to hide and no reason to be blind. It is an emergency for humanity, for only an emergency and a great need could propel God to send a New Revelation into the world.

The New Revelation will expose humanity's weakness and ignorance, its beliefs, its prejudices, its insistence that it knows God's Will. It will hide behind its rationality. It will hide behind its scriptures. It will hide behind its repudiation, its denial and its ambitions.

In a sense, the times to come are the fruits of humanity's labors—the bitter fruits of deception and conquest, of greed and ambition, of the misuse of the world. Humanity, who cannot control its passions, its population, its ambitions; humanity, who cannot think ahead for the future, who will use up everything right now, will spend its natural inheritance, thinking that it is endless and cannot be exhausted.

And what will humanity do? How will it adapt and survive? And what will it face in the universe around it, of which humanity knows nothing, projecting only its wishes and fantasies?

How will humanity find the strength and the commitment to cooperate and to unite for the preservation of civilization? How will humanity prepare for a Greater Community of life that is not human and that does not value the human spirit? And how will humanity determine its friends from its foes in the universe, as many come bearing gifts and secret plans? And how will the individual, how will you, find the real purpose that has brought you into the world—a purpose that exists beyond your intellect, your ideas and your plans and goals? And who will clarify religion to bring forth its essence, its fundamental teaching and purpose? Who can separate the gold from the dross? Who can see that humanity is at the great threshold of emerging into a universe that will be unlike anything that you can now comprehend?

If you are honest, you will see you do not have an answer to these questions. You do not even have an answer as to how you will find your true path and the strength to follow it. At this moment, there are only a few adept individuals, and even fewer teachers, who can offer you this, but they know nothing of humanity's future and the great change that is upon the world.

Here you must have humility and tremendous self-honesty, or you will think that you know when you do not know, and you will rely upon assumptions that have no basis in reality.

You will see all of this as the Messenger begins to emerge from obscurity, where he has been kept back for decades, receiving the New Message from God. You will see the denial. You will see the ridicule. You will see the disbelief and the repudiation.

People will cling to their old religion, afraid of what God might reveal now. Underneath all of this denial and rejection is fear—fear of life, fear of the future, fear of change, fear of Revelation.

People have committed so many grievous acts against themselves and others that they are now afraid that God might speak again. But they will hide this fear behind their pride and their assumptions and their beliefs. They will hide in their state houses and in their mosques, and in their temples and churches.

The Messenger today has no better chance of being received than the great Messengers of the past. His advantage is that his voice can be carried around the world. His benefit is that he has spent 25 years receiving the New Message from God in its pure form. And once presented, it cannot stop.

The power and the wisdom of this Message surpasses human understanding and will resonate at the deepest levels of the individual's heart and soul. But if people do not know their heart and soul, then the Message will not find its true recipients.

Humanity must repent. It must change. It is blindly following a path of self-destruction where it will be vulnerable not only to its own devastating behavior on Earth, but to intervention and manipulation from beyond. The Earth is too valuable for conquest, and so the attempt at control will be subtle and persuasive, speaking to humanity's greed and ignorance and superstitions.

It is this great vulnerability that the Prophet will speak of. He has been given the words and the Message. The Message is so great and huge and so encompassing that there will be no room for human confabulation and human invention and manipulation of the pure Message.

But it will take time. For people are dead to their own Knowledge, the deeper intelligence that God has placed within them. They are dead to themselves—driven, rushing about, feverishly trying to survive or to fulfill their desires, caught up in the drama of everyday life.

So the first to respond will be those who are feeling the stirring. They have been called already, but they do not know what they are being called for. They are discontented and distressed because they know there is something greater for them, but they cannot find it. They cannot find it in their culture, their religion, their family, their ideas. They cannot find it in politics or social movements. They are being stirred by the greater Power of God. They are preparing themselves for the Revelation, but they do not see this yet.

Humanity thinks one way, but life is moving another way. So the Prophet is speaking to the dead and to the dying, to the deaf, to the blind.

But his words will reach into the minds and hearts of those who have been stirred, who are not content to base their lives on old values and assumptions, old beliefs and institutions. They are being stirred to awaken out of a deep and dreadful slumber. The Prophet will speak to them. His Message will be presented to the world to call to them, for they will be the first to recognize and to respond to the Revelation.

The Prophet is not here to be exalted. He will not perform miracles to impress people. He will not be so sensational that people will be blinded by him, for that is all foolishness and has never been the case with God's real Messengers. Only the stories that were invented after the passing of the Messengers, after the Messengers were destroyed by their own people, their own cultures, were the fantastic tales created. But it is never the real life of the Messenger, you see.

The tales are created, the miracles are invented to persuade the unknowing, to intrigue those who cannot on their own recognize the reality of the Revelation.

Humanity has built up layer upon layer of belief and assumption that has nothing to do with the reality of the true life. Like the great temples of old, they have become encrusted, overlaid with beauty and decay. Where will the New Revelation then be received in such an environment?

Clearly, the Messenger alone cannot bring a New Message from God into the world, so those who are being stirred now must assist him. They must learn of the New Message. They must study it. They must apply it to their lives. They must take the Steps to Knowledge within themselves to find the greater voice and the power that God has given to them, which are waiting to be discovered.

The Messenger is here to empower people, to renew their ancient ties to Knowledge and to equip and prepare them for the Great Waves of change that are coming to the world.

There will be many voices who will speak of change. There will be many voices who will speak of prophecy. There are many voices who will project fearful or desirable images of the future. There will be many voices claiming to reveal a New Message from God. But there is only one, for this has always been the way that God has brought a New Revelation into the world.

If the Revelation were given to many people, there would be different versions. People would alter it. People would adapt it to their current thinking and beliefs, their current religion and culture, and the Message would lose its clarity, its integrity and its focus.

Only one who has been prepared to be the Messenger can be the Messenger. Only one who is called and prepared to be the Prophet for this time and this age can be the Prophet for this time and this age.

There are many bright people in the world who will reveal, through their own intelligence, a recognition of the world's condition and its future difficulties. But only the Prophet can reveal what it really means, and how it can be attended to and what must change at the deepest level of people's minds and hearts—to change course, to recognize reality and to prepare for a future that will be unlike anything they have ever known.

There will be many voices. Some of them will be charming and persuasive, elegant and articulate. But only the Messenger knows and has the true Message. Only he can deliver it, for only he has received it. Only he can embody it.

The burden, then, is upon the listener, the recipient. The test is for them. Will they remain blind, or will light begin to penetrate where there was only darkness before? Will they respond at the deeper level of Knowledge, or will they just project their attitudes and beliefs?

The Messenger has passed the test. He does not need to provide miracles to convince people because the miracle is the New Message itself, and the miracle is the power and presence of Knowledge within the individual.

If someone were to say, "Well, that is not good enough for me," then what they are saying is that they have no awareness; they are ignorant. But instead of admitting their ignorance, they will project themselves as knowing and competent to make such a judgment.

This is the further stupidity of humanity—a child now with power, a child now who is ruining the world and who is setting itself up to be manipulated and dominated by powerful and heartless forces in the universe.

God's New Message now is not simply for the unique individual or the rare and refined intelligence. It is not the providence of the elite, the rich and the powerful or the highly educated. It is for the people—to learn to recognize Knowledge and to follow Knowledge, and to receive the guidance and the counsel, the warning and the blessing of God's New Revelation.

You will see now, as time goes on, the great need for this Revelation and the great resistance to this Revelation. When something this pure is brought into the world, it will show everything that is impure and how the truth has been alloyed with convention and convenience, with ambition and corruption. The light will reveal the darkness and will reveal what everyone is hiding for themselves.

Do not fear God's condemnation, for God loves the world. And understand that without Knowledge, humanity can only be foolish and self-indulgent. There is no condemnation here. The angry God is the projection of the angry person. People want God to carry out the vengeance that they themselves seek. People want God to carry out justice that they themselves would prescribe.

But God is beyond these things. Why would human folly disturb the Creator of all the universes, the Creator of more races in the universe than your numbers could account for?

The tragedy is that humanity is not responding to God's Presence and communication. And as a result the human family is suffering and is taking a path of decline, conflict and self-destruction. There is not enough resident wisdom and restraint in the world yet to counteract these tremendous negative tendencies.

It is not the end of time. It is a great transition—a transition to a different kind of life in a different kind of world, a transition from living in isolation in the universe to living in a Greater Community of life, where humanity will have to create its own rules of engagement and protection for the world. It is a transition to a new and sustainable life in the world so that humanity can have a future. It is a transition of such great significance and impact that there is nothing in human history that can compare with it. Even the collapse of ancient civilizations, though dramatic and symbolic, cannot match the impact of the Great Waves of change that are coming to the world or humanity's encounter with a Greater Community of life.

Only the Messenger can speak of these things with real clarity, for he has been given the New Message from God. In obscurity, he has received it, and now he must present it and speak for it and call people to it. It is a tremendous and disheartening task.

So everyone who can respond is significant in receiving and learning and living the Revelation. Everyone can make the difference in whether human civilization will survive and grow or crumble under its own weight and dysfunction.

You must look forward. You must open your mind. Set aside your condemnation of others. Unburden yourself from the weight of history so that your eyes may be clear, so that your ears can hear and your heart may know.

God's New Message speaks of the present and the future. The past is only memories now. You carry wisdom from the past, and lessons from the past, and gratitude for the contribution of individuals and nations from the past, but you must be present now and look to the future. And the New Revelation will give you the eyes to see if you can receive it and learn of it with humility and gratitude.

The Prophet will need your assistance and support. And Knowledge within you will tell you how this can be done.

If you are to face the future without trepidation and denial, you must have this power and this presence within yourself, and that is why the New Message is for you. It is not here to replace the world's religions, but to give them a greater capacity, a greater awareness. Otherwise, they will become irrelevant in the future when humanity is facing its greatest trials.

The Prophet is not a personality. He is a vehicle for God's deliverance into the world. His personal life is only a platform. His personal interests are only the by-product of living in culture. But his personal awareness has been superseded by the Will and the Power of the Creator and God's Message for the world.

Few will understand him, but the recognition can occur. And those who can see will be blessed, and their lives will be justified, and their presence in the world will be acknowledged.

Those who can receive will be strengthened and given courage and confidence that they could not receive otherwise.

Those who can respond will understand themselves and their past and will be able to free themselves from self-hatred and unforgiveness.

Those who can receive will be illuminated over time, as they themselves take the Steps to Knowledge.

This is the great truth that must be recognized. You cannot recognize it with your intellect, for it is only full of thoughts from the past. It must be a deeper resonance through the Ancient Corridors of your mind. And those doors must be open now for you to see, to know and to receive for yourself and for all those who you may be able to serve and to assist in the future.

CHAPTER 11

THE CONSEQUENCE OF REVELATION

As revealed to
Marshall Vian Summers
on September 4, 2011
in Boulder, Colorado

If God were to speak to humanity only once in a millennium, surely it would have great consequence as to how it was received and what was done with it as a result. Surely these great interventions from the Divine mark great turning points in human history and the evolution of human awareness and thought and social engagement.

Such a time has come again, at this time of Revelation. And the consequences are great, for humanity is facing its greatest trials. It is facing a world of declining resources and growing population. It is facing the deterioration of your natural environment, and a disruption of the world's climate, and the great impacts this will have on your ability to grow food and to engage in transportation.

Humanity is facing its greatest trials. You stand at the threshold of a Greater Community of intelligent life in the universe, a non-human universe that does not value human awareness or human accomplishments. You are reaching a point where humanity must grow up and become responsible and united if it is to survive within its own world and remain free within this Greater Community, where freedom itself is rare.

It has taken such a great threshold to call a New Message from God into the world. And now God has spoken again, through God's

Messenger, delivering a Message more comprehensive and complete than anything that has ever been given to this world, given at a time of Revelation.

The hour is late. The consequences are significant. Humanity is facing a new world—a new world of environmental disruption, a new world of social and economic upheaval, a new world that will not be like the past, a new world that must be comprehended with fresh eyes, not with assumptions from the past. Even wisdom from the past may in cases be ineffective or inadequate to deal with the Great Waves of change that are coming to the world and that are striking the world even at this moment.

For humanity, it is a time of great reckoning—a time of collective responsibility, a time to end your ceaseless conflicts and your pathetic indulgences to face a far more difficult world and to face the reality of the Greater Community, of which humanity knows almost nothing at all.

It is because of this that God has spoken again and has sent a great Message into the world. But even the Creator of all life cannot assure or determine how this will be received here or how the Messenger will be regarded. For he is not here to substantiate past Revelations or to fulfill past prophecies, but instead to bring an entirely new awareness and understanding into the world—the great turning point, that even at this moment few can see and fewer still can understand.

People are anxious. They are afraid. They look nervously over the horizon. They know that times are uncertain and will grow ever more uncertain. Despite the assurances of your governments and institutions, the human heart is troubled, for there is a Greater Darkness in the world.

THE CONSEQUENCE OF REVELATION

It is a time of great consequence. Should the Revelation be denied or forestalled, should the Messenger be withheld or destroyed, it would have a great impact on the outcome for every person and for your children and their children as well.

In this respect, the Messenger is the most important person in the world, for his presence and the success or failure of his mission in bringing this greater awareness, this New Revelation, to humanity will have far greater impact than the decisions or the circumstances of any other person on Earth.

And yet the Messenger cannot assure his success. He has proven himself so far to be able to receive the Revelation, and now he is beginning to communicate it and to present it to the world. But this success cannot be on his shoulders, but must be shared amongst the many who can receive him, and the many who will respond to those who can receive him and so on and so forth.

If humanity can be alerted and prepared for the Great Waves of change and for the great hazards of contact with the universe, then humanity has the great possibility to build a future far better than its past—a future without incessant war and conflict, a future without degrading and overwhelming impoverishment and oppression, a future on a more barren planet of Earth, but a planet that is being wisely managed and sustained so that humanity may have a future here.

Do not think that you will leave to another world, for there is no inhabitable world within your vicinity, the closest being well inhabited by races far older than you. Do not think you can despoil your planet of origin and that God will provide you an alternative, for there is no alternative, you see.

Give up these fantasies, these ridiculous assumptions. Come to your senses, recognizing you are standing on a fragile world being degraded with each passing day. Realize you are facing a universe that you know nothing about—a universe full of intelligent life, a greater reality, a competitive reality on a scale you cannot even imagine.

Do not think your technology will save you. Do not think that Jesus will return, or the Imam or the Maitreya. For God has sent a New Messenger into the world. He is not here to fulfill the past, but to prepare humanity for its future and its destiny.

If his voice is ignored, if he is too greatly resisted, if enough people cannot receive and respond to the New Message, then humanity will continue [towards] its desperate and predictable future, its path towards incremental self-destruction, its path away from its greater destiny, facing collapse within the world and subjugation from forces from beyond the world—things that humanity as a whole is barely aware of, if at all.

It is a very grave situation, but the Creator loves humanity and has sent a blessing, a warning and a preparation. It has been given to one man to receive—a man who was prepared for this role before he came, a man sent here by the Angelic Presence, a humble man, a simple man, a man without social position, a man who has spent the last 40 years preparing and receiving the Revelation.

He will be attacked. He will be denied. He will be avoided. He will be ridiculed. For this always happens at times of Revelation.

While the world celebrates its heroes and its heroines, the Messengers go unrecognized. They who have the greatest power to alter the course of humanity are barely recognized by anyone.

You are living now at such a time—a momentous time, a time of great promise, a time of great possibility, a time of dire circumstances and grave human error, a time when you must be strengthened and the presence of Knowledge, the deeper intelligence that God has given you, is to be renewed so that you will have the courage and the determination to face a new world, so that you will have the orientation you need to prepare for the Greater Community.

Such things cannot be left up to secret governments or secret groups or elite organizations because it is the world that must be prepared, or humanity's future freedom and sovereignty can be given away—traded away for technology, traded away on a mere promise of peace and prosperity, given away by selfish interests who have not the wisdom to comprehend who they are dealing with and what course of action they really must take.

The Messenger is here to give humanity the one thing, the one missing ingredient—the power and the presence within each person that must be ignited if they are to awaken from their troubled sleep of fear, tragedy and desire. It is the one thing that will awaken people to their greater purpose, but it must be given from the Creator. It is not something humanity can do on its own. It must be shown. It must be activated. For you cannot lift yourself up without this power and this activation.

If humanity should fail the Revelation, your world will continue to decline—destroying not only individuals but whole nations of people; setting you into war and contest over who will have the remaining resources; a situation far more grave, grievous and tragic than anything humanity has ever faced before.

And into this growing chaos, forces coming from the universe will arrive, promising peace, prosperity and high technology. They will come offering gifts with their secret plans—plans that have been long in formation, long considered. You will think they are wondrous, almost divine, but it is all a ruse. It is all a deception to weaken humanity.

What discernment will it [humanity] have when it is desperate, when it has driven itself into desperation? What wisdom will it have? Its seers will be denied or neglected.

The outcome is predictable. It has happened countless times in the universe when a nation outstrips the wealth of its world, falls into depletion and despair, only to be taken up by foreign powers—not through violent conquest, but through inducement and seduction.

If you knew anything about the Greater Community, you would understand this. But humanity knows nothing of the Greater Community. How could it know, isolated here in this world? To you, the universe is full of fantasy and fear. You are enamored with its possibilities. You are terrified of its realities.

That is why the Revelation must provide the reality and spirituality of the Greater Community, to reveal to you what life is really like in this region of space—what you can expect, how you should conduct yourself, when and where engagement should take place and under what circumstances. Otherwise, you will be the ignorant and easily seduced natives of the new world, falling prey to seduction or frightened into submitting yourself and thereby undoing your entire culture and reality.

This is the great warning, and it must be heeded, or you will not understand the blessing and the preparation. It is time to grow up and become serious about your life and your purpose and the meaning of your existence here.

The rich indulge themselves endlessly—in their hobbies, their passions and their plays while the rest of the world sinks into despair, poverty and degradation. Surely, this cannot be a world that will survive as a free race in the universe. Surely, this is a race that will not have the collective wisdom to restrain its activities and to prepare for its future. Surely, this will be an easy prize for those who use cunning and guile to achieve their goals.

For the world is rich. You do not understand how rich it really is, how precious it is in a universe of barren worlds. You know not of the value of this world nor the meaning of your presence here at this time—a time of Revelation.

The Messenger is burdened with this, to communicate all these things and much more. For the Revelation speaks on almost every aspect of your life, giving you strength and promise, clarity and integrity, lifting the veil of ignorance, releasing you from the chains of fear and anxiety and self-recrimination.

It is a fabulous gift, more precious than you can realize at the outset. And as the world grows darker, this gift will become more recognized. As the threat to human freedom and well-being escalates, the Revelation begins to reveal its greater promise.

At the outset, there will be those who are unsettled already, who have not been able to commit themselves to the great religious traditions of the past, who are not complacent with the way things appear to be, who are not satisfied with little pleasures and great pains, who have the prescience and the humility to respond to a New Revelation. Their numbers will be few at the outset, but this has always been the case at times of Revelation.

People do not want to face a Revelation from God. They think it will be a punishment. They think it will be a set of demands. They are so guilty from their misbehavior, their crimes against themselves and one another, they do not want to hear what God would have to say. They will fear retribution. They will fear condemnation.

But what God gives is the great Love and the great Wisdom and the preparation at this great turning point so that humanity can face and begin to prepare for a new world reality and for the reality of the Greater Community.

God has given you the eyes to see and the ears to hear, but you are still deaf and blind. For you have not responded to Knowledge in your life sufficiently yet to be able to see it clearly and to hear the truth amidst all that is pleasing and promising and seductive.

But you can take the Steps to Knowledge and regain this power and this strength, for the world requires it now. It is not merely for your personal edification, or your personal enhancement or your personal enlightenment. It is really to play a part at a great turning point for humanity, the small but essential part that you must play.

Do not think God is going to intervene and save the world in the last hour. For God has sent you and everyone else to save the world before there is a last hour.

But this mission and this purpose are not reflected in your personal wishes and goals. You must respond to a deeper voice within you and the Voice of Revelation that is presenting God's New Message for the world.

THE CONSEQUENCE OF REVELATION

It is so hard to trust that something is so pure, so powerful and so significant when the world has shown you what is so corrupt, what is so degraded, what is so deceiving and disappointing.

But God has given you the eyes to see and the ears to hear. You will know that the Revelation is true, and the more that you immerse yourself in it, the truer it will become. For it will resonate with the truth of your own Being even if it does not conform to your ideas or beliefs or expectations.

But, you see, your ideas, your beliefs and your expectations do not even allow you to see the new world you are entering and are living in already. They do not allow you to see the reality of the Greater Community or even that there is a Greater Community or that this would be in any way important for your life.

It is your beliefs and your attitudes and your preferences that blind you and disable you from hearing the greater voice within yourself and within others. Accept this as your condition, and your starting point will be honest. And your response will have the possibility of being genuine and efficacious.

God has spoken again. The Revelation is in the world. The Messenger is here. What could be more consequential than this? What could have a greater impact on your life and future, and the life and future of your children than this?

Look ahead. What do you see in the world? Yes, you are afraid because what you see will make you afraid, and you will feel ineffectual in the face of it.

God must strengthen you and unburden you and revive you and return you to a state of integrity so that you may become powerful and effective in contributing to a world in need, so that your gifts may be recognized and rendered where they are meant to be rendered. For this is the foundation for fulfillment in the world.

Knowledge within you cannot be destroyed. It is the part of you that cannot be destroyed, and so it is without fear. But it is here on a mission, which is your mission—the mission which has brought you to the world. You are not merely here to consume and to survive and to be gratified. You are really here for a greater purpose, and those who sent you are watching you now.

The consequence of your response to the Revelation is all-important in determining the outcome for you and whether your great and difficult journey in the world will be successful and fulfilling.

You must face the great needs of the world and realize that humanity alone cannot resolve them. There is not enough collective wisdom or conscientiousness here yet for humanity to do that. There are inspired individuals. There are individuals who are committed to service, but their numbers are too small, and they cannot hold sway over the passions and grievances of humanity. That is why the Revelation must be given to as many people as possible.

And those who are ready, who have been stirred, they will respond. The Messenger will not have to produce miracles for them, for the Revelation is the miracle, and their ability to respond to Revelation is the miracle. What greater miracle could there be than this? Some kind of phenomenon or trick?

Those who are intervening in your world from the Greater Community can create phenomena and tricks. They can make you think that they are divine and that you must follow them without question. With Knowledge, you would not do this, and you would see the deception. But many are not with Knowledge though it lives within them at this moment.

The acceptance or the denial of the Revelation will be of the greatest consequence for the future of humanity and for the outcome of your life. But you must see this with your own eyes and hear this with your own heart and soul. Our words may not be enough. Even the Messenger being in the world may not be enough.

And that is why the Message is being given to the individual, with the emphasis on the individual, and not taken to the corridors of power, where everything becomes manipulated and corrupted.

God has spoken again. The Messenger is in the world. You are blessed to live at a time of Revelation. The great promise is before you.

It is this consequence for you and your life and then beyond you for others and for the world that is the most important thing. It is your ability to respond—your responsibility—that is the most important thing. You do not need to be perfect. You do not need to be at peace at all times, for that will not happen, not if you are responsible and honest about your life.

The Message is pure. It will reveal all human deception, corruption, denial and intrigue. Your response must be pure. Beyond the realm of your intellect it will be, in a whole other part of you that you know very little about.

It is the response that will determine the outcome. If humanity cannot prepare for the Greater Community, its freedom and sovereignty will be lost. It will be lost if humanity cannot prepare for the Great Waves of change, if nations cannot unite for their own preservation and support each other to maintain balance and harmony, stability and security in the world.

It is your weakness that will be preyed upon. It is the breakdown of human civilization that will be the opportunity for others to intervene. You must see this with new eyes, without condemnation.

God cannot change human perception, but God has given you Knowledge that is not bound by human perception. And this can arise in your awareness—this power, this grace, this presence. That is the great redemption for you, and that is what will give humanity the clarity, the wisdom and the power to take the actions it must take to secure the world and prepare for its future in the Greater Community as a free and self-determined race.

May the gift be with you, for the gift is with you. But you cannot call it out of yourself. It must be called out of you from a Greater Power, and that Calling is the Creator calling to you as part of Creation. And your response will be a response to this—the most important communication of your life.

CHAPTER 12

THE MESSENGER'S CALLING

As revealed to
Marshall Vian Summers
on September 3, 2014
in Boulder, Colorado

God has sent a Messenger into the world, sent from the Angelic Assembly he is. He is the first Messenger to come since the days of Muhammad. And another will not be sent for a very long time.

His role is so important. He is bringing something into the world that has never been brought here before, continuing the great series of Revelations brought to humanity at critical turning points in its history and evolution.

He comes at a time of great and growing need as humanity is facing a world of immense environmental change, and all of the political and economic upheaval that will result. He is coming at a time when humanity stands at the threshold of a universe full of intelligent life. He comes at a time when humanity must prepare.

His calling to the world is that the world must receive this. People of all nations, cultures and religious affiliations, he is calling to you—for those who can hear, for those who can receive, for those who realize that a New Revelation must come.

For religion has fallen into disarray and is conflicted within itself and between its primary expressions. It has become a tool of the state and a tool of those who seek power and domination over others.

And yet this alone has not brought the New Revelation into the world. It is indeed the great threshold that humanity is facing, that only the New Message from God can fully reveal to you. It is a threshold of immense change in the world, which will require preparation and adaptation on a scale never seen before. It will require preparation for humanity's engagement with life in the universe, which has already begun, but in a way that is highly dangerous for the human family.

People of all nations, cultures and religious traditions, the Messenger is calling for you to have the courage and the honesty to feel the great need to have God speak to you once again. For God only speaks to humanity at great turning points, at times of great need and opportunity.

The sincere prayers and the requests and true needs of people all around the world are being met now through the Revelation. But God does not give people what they expect. God gives people what they need for this time and for the times to come. And the Revelations are so vast and deep that they speak to the needs of people yet to be born, the peoples fifty years from now or two hundred years from now—so great is the Revelation. That is why God's previous Revelations have grown in time and were able to provide continuously for the people of different eras and different nations, in all manner of circumstances.

Such will be the case with God's New Revelation if it can be received and accepted, studied and applied. It is not here to replace the world's religions, but to give them greater scope and dimension and to unite them. For they were all initiated by God, and they have all been changed by man through adoption, through confusion and through corruption.

People of all nations, cultures and religious traditions, the Messenger is calling for you to recognize your deeper need, the need of your soul. This is not just the need of the day, or the events of the world, or the crisis of this moment. It is a need that is more pervasive and deep—the need to be reunited with your Source, the need to gain the strength that only Heaven can provide, the need to know your true purpose and direction beyond what your culture, and even your religion, have prescribed for you. For only God can give you this.

The need to forgive, the need for integrity, the need for true purpose and direction beyond what your culture and others have prescribed for you—this must come from God if it is to be true and efficacious, if it is to serve you in all times, in all manner of situations—beyond all the divisions of humanity, beyond all the conflicts of humanity, beyond all the failures of humanity.

God knows what is coming over the horizon and seeks to warn you, to bless you and to prepare you.

The Messenger now is calling for you to hear, to respond, to find this, to receive this, to set aside your judgments and your preferences and your admonitions so that you can receive the blessings of the Creator, given anew now under a very different set of circumstances, as humanity is about to face its greatest trials.

Not everyone will be able to respond at first, but there are many in the world today who are ready to hear this. From all nations, all cultures, from all faith traditions, there are many who are ready to hear this calling.

The Messenger is an older man now. So time is of the essence for you to hear him, for you to receive him and for you to recognize him in his remaining years on Earth.

He is calling to you to receive, to learn and to take the Steps to Knowledge, the deeper knowledge that God has placed within you that was placed within you before you even came into the world—to guide you, to protect you and to lead you to a greater life of purpose and fulfillment in the world. You cannot give yourself these things.

Without this Knowledge, people will follow the tribe. They will follow the culture. They will follow the admonitions of others. They will become lost in a world of desire, fantasy and grievance. They will live lives of desperation and often violence. They will be unprepared for the greater forces that are changing the world even at this moment.

Without Knowledge, people will be set against each other as they always have—struggling, competing, fighting, destroying one another as they always have.

It is only because of the great Messengers and Messages that humanity has even come this far with so much success, despite its many failures and errors.

But now a New Revelation must be given. The Messenger has spent 40 years receiving it in isolation. He must now proclaim to the world in his remaining years. His calling, then, is not just to one group or one nation or one region. It is to the whole world, and that is why he is broadcasting to the whole world, and providing the Revelation to the whole world, and providing for the first time in all of human history the Voice of Revelation.

Such a Voice that spoke to the Jesus, the Buddha and the Muhammad you can hear for the first time—Our Voice, this Voice, the Voice of the Angelic Assembly speaking together all as one, a reality and phenomenon your intellect cannot fathom, but which your heart can receive powerfully.

For the Lord is the Lord of the entire universe, with countless races of beings so unlike you, and other dimensions of the physical universe and of Creation beyond the physical realm entirely.

God has put Knowledge within you. Should you awaken to this and become responsive to this, then God's Will can move you and protect you and guide you, for you need this now more than ever before.

People of all nations, cultures and religious traditions, hear the Messenger's calling [to] you. Do not dispute this. Do not deny this, or you deny God's Grace and Power. And you deny God's gift to you, which you need now more than anything.

For the great traditions of the past cannot prepare humanity for the great change that is coming to the world or for humanity's encounter with intelligent life in the universe—the two greatest events in all of human history, the two events that, more than anything else, can affect the future of every person on Earth and those yet to come. So great is the need you can barely recognize it. It is beyond the needs that you think of.

But the world is beginning to break down. Human civilization is beginning to break down. It will affect you and every person, rich or poor, in every country, in every corner of the world.

You must hear the Messenger's call to you. God has sent him here to be the recipient and the primary representative of God's New Revelation for the world.

Do not dispute this on religious grounds. For you cannot determine what God will do or when God will speak. You cannot determine that another Messenger cannot be sent into the world. Only arrogance and foolishness would make such proclamations.

You are entering a new world of diminishing resources, violent weather, failing crops and immense biological and physical change in the world created by humanity's foolishness, greed and misuse of the world. It is a time of growing need, escalating with each passing day. Few people are aware of what this would really mean and how much it would change their circumstances. But God knows, and the Revelation reveals this very clearly.

What person in the world knows what life in the universe is, or what encounters of this nature would require or mean for humanity, and how to tell friend from foe in such an encounter? Only God knows, and God has sent the Revelation to reveal this to you and to prepare you for this, for nothing in the world can prepare you for this.

People of all nations, cultures and religious traditions, hear the Messenger's call. He is the one person who can do this. For he has been sent from the Angelic Assembly. He is no ordinary person. He is not a God, for no person is a God. But he is a member of the Assembly and he is in world. For all the great Messengers have come from the Assembly. That is what has given them the power and the association to bring the great Revelations that they have brought into the world.

Now you are living at a time of Revelation. It is a time that will challenge your faith, your courage, your confidence, your trust in yourself and in others in ways never seen before. Even the great wars of the past century will mean very little compared with what you will be facing now—the product of humanity's misuse of the world.

Only God can show you the way. For so far, humanity on its own has not been able to correct its behavior. Only God can show you a path to a greater future for the human family, for people cannot invent this for themselves.

For this, you must see that God is much greater than you previously thought—a God of countless races in the universe, a God of a realm of life so expansive that your intellect can hardly fathom it, or [even any] part of it.

This is the God who has sent you into the world through your Spiritual Family. This is the God that has put Knowledge within you to guide you and to give you Wisdom from beyond the world. This is the God who will return to you your true integrity, your deeper nature and the real purpose that has brought you into the world under the very circumstances that you seek to deny or to avoid.

People of all nations, cultures and faith traditions, hear the Messenger's call, for it is the Calling of God. He is the Messenger. But he is not merely here to deliver the Message, but to represent it and to speak for it. It is because of who he is and where he has come from that makes this possible.

There is no one else in the world who could seize God's Revelation and use it for themselves, for they have not the power or the connection to do this. And Heaven will not honor them, no matter what they proclaim for themselves.

Only one has been sent. For this is the way of things. Only one has been sent, and he is in the world, and he is calling to you. He is calling to you in his voice, and he is calling to you through the Revelation itself, which is being made available to the world as quickly as possible.

The Messenger is a humble man. He has no position in the world. He has been through a preparation unlike anything you can imagine for a greater calling and a greater mission here on Earth. But he must speak to the people of Earth and reach as many as he can in his remaining years.

This is his calling to you. This is your challenge. Can you face the Light of Revelation? Can you be receptive to God's New Revelation for the world? Can you take it to heart and apply it in your life? For it will provide so much for you right now, in everything you are doing and everything you need.

God has given the Revelation for the world, and yet it provides the restoration for each person who can receive it and apply it in their lives. Only the genius of the Creator could do this. Only the genius of the Creator could speak to people of every nation, every culture and every faith tradition through the New Revelation.

The blessing is upon you. The Messenger is calling for you to receive it. The Messenger is calling for you to be truly honest and receptive. The Messenger is calling for you to set aside your beliefs and your admonitions so that you can be receptive to the Revelation. If you cannot do this, then God cannot help you. God cannot assist you.

For God is still present in the world, and God's Revelation to humanity has now come again.

CHAPTER 13

WALKING WITH THE MESSENGER

As revealed to
Marshall Vian Summers
on October 21, 2012
in Kuala Lumpur, Malaysia

Everyone who can receive the Revelation, in humility and honesty, will be walking with the Messenger. In some degree, either great or small, they will be doing what he is doing. They will be following the pathway that he is blazing for everyone.

Any true student will do this naturally because they are following Knowledge, and they are taking the Steps to Knowledge, and they are building a strong foundation for their greater and future life through the Four Pillars of development—the Pillar of Relationships, the Pillar of Work and Providership, the Pillar of Health and the Pillar of Spiritual Development.

To walk with the Messenger is to understand the Revelation as it is pertaining to your own life and to the lives of those whom you will influence.

It is a great calling, you see, but before you can give, you must receive, and you must prepare, for you are not ready for your greater life. You are not ready for your greater purpose, which has been waiting so long for you to begin.

First, you must allow Knowledge to rearrange your life, to bring harmony and balance there, integrity, purpose and meaning. And this will take time, for there are certain things that must be undone and certain things that must be initiated and sustained.

Most people are not yet able to carry out such a great preparation on their behalf and on the behalf of others, both seen and unseen, who are depending upon their development.

At the beginning, people think the journey is all about them and their happiness and contentment, but it is really about something greater than these things. And they will discover as they proceed that they are learning not only for themselves but for others and, in their own small way, for the entire world.

For God wills that humanity now learn a Greater Community Way of Knowledge.

God wills that humanity join together out of great necessity and urgency to preserve human civilization in the face of great change that is coming to the world.

God wills that humanity prepare for its future and destiny within a Greater Community of intelligent life in the universe.

God wills that the religions cooperate with one another, for they are all born of the same Source. And, ultimately, if correctly understood in the Light of the New Revelation, they all serve the same purpose and outcome, which is to keep Knowledge alive in the world, to give people the opportunity to discover their greater life and purpose within the circumstances of the world.

Here you must see that your destiny is connected with the Messenger himself, for he is bringing the Revelation that will reveal your greater destiny and its possibilities for the future.

For, you see, destiny is everything, for everyone was sent into the world for a higher purpose. If their purpose can be discovered and fulfilled sufficiently, then someone is fulfilling their greater destiny.

But, alas, most people have not found this, and they have built lives that are not oriented towards this. They are lost in the world— lost and forlorn. Even if they are wealthy, even if they have all the privileges that everyone seeks, they are lost and forlorn. Their lives are empty. They cannot be fulfilled.

For only Knowledge can fulfill your life, and Knowledge comes from God. And Knowledge is connected to your purpose and your destiny. And your destiny is connected to those people who will share in its particular expression.

But when a Messenger comes into the world, you see, it sets the direction of the destiny of many, many people, either directly or indirectly. To think apart from this is to miss one of the critical ingredients to your self-revelation. For this is what draws you out of Separation, you see: to realize that the sacred relationships of your life create the context and the meaning of your life and that these relationships were destined before you came. How you will find them, and if you will find them, is dependent upon many circumstances here on Earth.

But you cannot change the reality of your destiny. You cannot change the meaning of your destiny. You cannot alter it to meet your objectives, your goals, your preferences.

To walk with the Messenger consciously, then, begins to allow you to resonate with this greater purpose, which will give you a sense of encouragement, courage and strength that nothing else can provide.

For these things now are connected to your destiny and not to other ambitions or activities.

To receive the Revelation is to walk with the Messenger. To walk with the Messenger is to receive the Revelation.

Though he will not be in the world forever, to learn of him in his life is an essential relationship for you now. For he is the bringer of God's New Word and Teaching for the world. He is the seed of Greater Community Knowledge and Wisdom in the world. There is no one else who can do this for the world.

In this light, Heaven looks upon him as the great hope for humanity, and all who associate with him and share his destiny as the greatest hope for humanity. Though there are other hopeful individuals and other great movements in the world, nothing is as essential to humanity's future—future well-being, future success, future redemption—as this.

Here all of the religions of the world will be involved. Here everything that is good will be involved. Everything that has been created that is beneficial will be involved. Everyone who feels a genuine calling will be called and influenced and affected if they can have the opportunity to receive and experience the Revelation.

There is no point in defending one's religious beliefs if it prevents you from receiving the Word of God for this time and for the times to come.

Those who are humble in the Light of Revelation will demonstrate their humility and their reverence. But those who lack this humility will struggle and fight, thinking that their ideas and their beliefs are the truth when, in fact, they are only approximations to a truth that far extends beyond them and their understanding.

To walk with the Messenger is to live as the Messenger lives, to receive and adopt the Revelation and all that it provides in every aspect of your life. It is to recognize you are part of something very great. Even at this moment, at a time of its very humble beginning, even without recognition from the world, even without prestige—without great monuments, without great ceremonies, without the deference of people everywhere—you are part of something at the beginning, at the outset.

And in these sacred years of the life of the Messenger, who will be his companions? Who will be his assistants? Who will receive the gift from him and share it with others?

This is a time of Revelation, you see. It only comes once in a millennium, and you are living at such a time. Does this not shed light on your greater purpose in the world? Does this not have relevance to why you were sent and what you are here to ultimately accomplish? Does this not connect with Knowledge within you, which is connected to Knowledge in the universe and to the Creator, which is its Source?

Even if you are alone in receiving the Revelation, you are part of its reality as you proceed. And this reality will grow for you naturally, for it emanates from within you outwardly—adjusting your outer life, affecting your values and priorities, giving you a deeper confidence and a greater strength.

Even if you are just beginning, it is a great opportunity for you. It is a blessing, indeed. You cannot yet see how complete this blessing really is at the outset, and perhaps not for a long time as you proceed, as you struggle with yourself—the opposition within yourself that has created the Separation for you and the opposition in the world that holds people back from receiving the Grace and the Power of the Creator, as it is now expressing itself in a radically changing world.

You must take the Steps to Knowledge, then, or these things will only be a belief and an idea, which you will either agree with or argue against. But you have not yet connected with the reality of the Revelation, so you do not know. And your rejection is born of ignorance and fear, and your acceptance is not yet authentic, for the reality is not yet strong enough within you to show you its meaning, its purpose and its immense value for your life.

Not everyone will have to receive God's New Revelation, but a great number of people will, around the world, for it to take residence here in the minds and hearts of people and then begin to radiate its wisdom, its power and its efficacy even to those who cannot receive it, to those who have not learned of it, to those in great need, to those who are stricken with poverty and oppression, to those who lead the world's governments and great enterprises and to everyone in between.

The wisdom and power of the Revelation will extend outwards, moving through the minds and hearts of people, borne now [by] those who share the destiny given by the Messenger in his time on Earth, given by the Revelation for all time, given for the value and the discovery of people everywhere, both now and in the future.

Those who walk with the Messenger in his time on Earth will be considered so fortunate to have this opportunity by all those in the future who will not be present at this time, or who cannot respond at this time.

You cannot yet see this, for you are lost in the world and cannot see the greater meaning that is now being given to the world. So you will have to listen, and consider, and open yourself to the Revelation so that it may reveal itself to you within your own experience. Then the reality of it will arise naturally, for it comes from the most natural place within you.

To walk with the Messenger is to face the adversity that he will have to face in bringing a New Revelation into the world—into a world of contentiousness and conflict, fear, doubt and aggravation; into a world where even the religions now are polarized against one another and are used for political purposes, generating conflict, contention and violence.

As the resources of the world decline in the future, these conflicts will become more severe, and people will be more polarized within their nations and between their nations. What will then be able to overcome these ever-growing difficulties and the great danger of war that they will produce, but the Light of Revelation itself that will restrain these activities and intentions and activate a recognition that all people in the world must now work for the preservation of civilization and for the well-being of the world so that it may emerge into this Greater Community of life as a free and self-determined people?

If you could recognize the great challenges ahead and the adversity you will have to face, you would see the importance of your life, and the importance of the Revelation, and the meaning of the Messenger walking the world, and your opportunity to walk with him.

But you must have the strength of Knowledge and the reality of the Revelation to give you the courage to face such great and monumental tasks, knowing that you will play your small but essential part, and that if enough people can respond, then humanity's future becomes ever more hopeful, ever more beneficial. The chance that you may escape the great attraction of war and conflict will grow and overcome these tendencies sufficiently that humanity may cross this great threshold into a new world, a new life and a greater future.

It is the great Love of the Creator, at the time of great peril, that makes all of this possible. Even if it seems impossible, even if you cannot see a way, even if everything seems to work against this, Knowledge will carry you forth to follow your journey, to walk in the Light of Revelation.

This [Knowledge] is the power beyond all powers. This is the strength beyond all strengths. This is the courage beyond all courage. This is the power, strength and courage that does not evoke conflict and war. It is not hateful. It does not contain revenge. It is not arrogant and ignorant. It does not put people in positions of higher authority beyond everyone else. It gives everyone authority according to their nature and purpose and design in the world at this time.

It will take many people strong with Knowledge to turn the tide for humanity. And they will have to be in concert with each other sufficiently for their efforts to gain strength and collaboration.

This is for you, you see. This is all about you and why you have come. It is not a philosophy. It is not just another approach. It is not a teaching amongst many teachings. It is *the* Teaching for this era and this time. Such a great claim can only be substantiated by such a great Teaching, and will only be known to you as you receive the gift of Revelation—its practices, its vision and its reality.

The Messenger's task is very difficult. It has taken him years to prepare for it, as it has taken him 40 years to receive the Revelation. Forty years, so that you could have a chance, so that your great opportunity could emerge, so that there would be a greater hope for humanity, so that humanity could be prepared for the great change that is coming to the world and for its difficult encounter with intelligent life in the universe.

It has been the Messenger's life and the life of others who joined him early to assist him in receiving this great promise for humanity. The Messenger cannot do this alone. Others must walk with him and speak for him and share the Revelation with him.

Everyone now is called into a greater service, you see, for the great times are upon you. And from here on, nothing will seem normal or stable in the world around you as you begin to enter the foothills of the Great Waves of change.

You will need this inner strength to maintain your balance as the waters become more turbulent, as your ship sways to and fro, as uncertainty arises around you and hostility and anger amongst many peoples. You will need a greater compass, a greater barometer, a greater ballast to hold your life steady in the turbulent times to come.

To share this is to walk with the Messenger and to keep him in your mind. For he is here to serve you, and you are here to serve him, not personally, but in a great effort to save humanity from the unknown calamities that it now faces and will face increasingly as the time continues.

What pulls you out of the hazard and the tragedy of your Separation is the Revelation and its reality. What restores to you your own integrity, your strength, your courage and your determination is the power of Knowledge within you, which God has given you for this time and set of circumstances.

It is your great relationships that are far more important than your ideas, your beliefs or anything your intellect can create and assemble. Do not think a great ideology can withstand the great change that is coming to the world. Do not think that a beautiful theology can withstand the harshness and the demands of a changing world. Do not think good intentions alone have the strength to overcome the fear and uncertainty you will see around you, and even within yourself.

This is a calling to be strong, to be determined, to outgrow little things, to set aside little passions, to build a greater strength and foundation in the Four Pillars of your life. This is what the Messenger does. This is what he asks you to do—for yourself and for others and for the world as a whole. This is the strength that others will not have. This is the clarity that others will not have. This is the certainty that others will not have. So who shall give it to them? How will it be shared in a world of increasing anxiety, uncertainty and conflict?

This is your question, and questions, to consider and ask for yourself. For it is by no accident that you have learned of the Revelation. It was intended to be, you see, because it is part of your destiny. Even if you are critical of it, even if you are unsure, even if you are suspicious, thinking it is like something else that was deceptive in the past, it is by no accident that you have come upon this during the time of the Messenger.

Someday he will pass from this world, and his wisdom will be saved and recorded for humanity. But even greater than the Messenger is the Message itself, which has been given with great care, with much repetition, with great clarity and demonstration so that it cannot be confused with other things. And you must not align the New Revelation with other things, for it represents a new beginning in your understanding, and the beginning of a new life for you.

Such is its power and meaning now. Such will be the need for it in the future. For your old life will fall prey to the discord of the world. Your old position will be vulnerable. Your old attitudes and ideas can work against you in the changing world around you.

You will need a new life for a new world. Nothing less, you see. This will bring new relationships to you and restore old ones that can be restored.

This is part of the gift of the Messenger for you. For he brings not only the Message, but he lives the Message and demonstrates the Message, and has passed through many of the adversities and uncertainties that you will encounter along the way and are possibly encountering even at this moment.

Let Us give blessing, then, to all who can walk with the Messenger and share in this reality, and amplify it for their own restoration, and for the gift that they are meant to give to others in the world who seek to reclaim their dignity, their strength, their courage and their true direction in life.

This is the greater life and greater promise, and it will not arise under normal circumstances, for nothing great arises under normal circumstances. Seek the peaceful, quiet, comfortable life, and your inner life will never emerge. Seek happiness only, and you will be deceived. And you will miss your great opportunity to give your gifts to a world in need.

It is the adversities of the world that will call this out of you and will convince you that there is no other alternative. There is no escape. There is no escaping into fantasy, or pursuits of happiness, or living some kind of idealized life in a world that is now beginning to undermine the safety and security of all of human civilization.

When you see this, finally, and have the courage to face this, you will recognize that you must rise to this great occasion. And you will recognize the Revelation as God providing the means and the vision for you to do this.

May the blessings of Heaven be upon you and all those who can walk with the Messenger—in understanding, in spirit, in feeling, to give strength to the Revelation and promise to your life, for they are one and the same.

IMPORTANT TERMS

$\mathcal{T}$he New Message from God reveals that our world stands at the greatest threshold in the history and evolution of humanity. At this threshold, a New Message from God has come. It reveals the great change that is coming to the world and our destiny within the Greater Community of life beyond our world, for which we are unaware and unprepared

Here the Revelation redefines certain familiar terms, but within a greater context and introduces other terms that are new to the human family. It is important to understand these terms when reading the texts of the New Message.

GOD is revealed in the New Message as the Source and Creator of all life and of countless races in the universe. Here the greater reality of God is unveiled in the expanded context of all life in this world and all life in the universe. This greater context redefines the meaning of our understanding of God and of God's Power and Presence in our lives. The New Message states that to understand what God is doing in our world, we must understand what God is doing in the entire universe. This understanding is now being revealed for the first time through a New Message from God. In the New Message, God is not a personage or a singular awareness, but instead a pervasive force and reality that permeates all life, existing beyond the limited boundaries of all theology and religious understanding. God speaks to the deepest part of each person through the power of Knowledge that lives within them.

THE SEPARATION is the ongoing state and condition of being separate from God. The Separation began when part of Creation willed to have the freedom to be apart from God, to live in a state of Separation. As a result, God created our evolving world and the expanding universe as a place for the separated to live in countless forms and places. Before the Separation, all life was in a timeless state of pure union. It is to this original state of union with God that all those living in Separation are ultimately called to return—through service, contribution and the discovery of Knowledge. It is God's mission in our world and throughout the universe to reclaim the separated through Knowledge, which is the part of each individual still connected to God.

KNOWLEDGE is the deeper spiritual mind and intelligence within each person, waiting to be discovered. Knowledge represents the eternal part of us that has never left God. The New Message speaks of Knowledge as the great hope for humanity, an inner power at the heart of each person that God's New Message is here to reveal and to call forth. Knowledge exists beyond the intellect. It alone has the power to guide each of us to our higher purpose and destined relationships in life.

THE ANGELIC ASSEMBLY is the great Angelic Presence that watches over the world. This Assembly is part of the hierarchy of service and relationship established by God to oversee the redemption and return of all separate life in the universe. Every world where sentient life exists is watched over by an Angelic Assembly. The Assembly overseeing our world has translated the Will of God for our time into human language and understanding, which is now revealed through the New Message from God. The term Angelic Assembly is synonymous with the terms Angelic Presence and Angelic Host.

THE NEW MESSAGE FROM GOD is an original Revelation and communication from God to the people of the world, both for our time and the times to come. The New Message is a gift from the

Creator of all life to people of all nations and religions and represents
the next great expression of God's Will and Plan for the human
family. The New Message is over 9000 pages in length and is the
largest Revelation ever given to the world, given now to a literate
world of global communication and growing global awareness. The
New Message is not an offshoot or reformation of any past tradition.
It is a New Message from God for humanity, which now faces great
instability and upheaval in the world and the great threshold of
emerging into a Greater Community of intelligent life in the universe.

THE VOICE OF REVELATION is the united voice of the Angelic
Assembly, delivering God's Message through a Messenger sent into
the world for this task. Here the Assembly speaks as one Voice, the
many speaking as one. For the very first time in history, you are
able to hear the actual Voice of Revelation speaking through God's
Messenger. It is this Voice that has spoken to all God's Messengers in
the past. The Word and the Sound of the Voice of Revelation are in
the world anew.

THE MESSENGER is the one chosen, prepared and sent into the
world by the Angelic Assembly to receive the New Message from
God. The Messenger for this time is Marshall Vian Summers. He is
a humble man with no position in the world who has undergone a
long and difficult preparation to be able to fulfill such an important
role and mission in life. He is charged with a great burden, blessing
and responsibility to receive God's pure Revelation and to protect and
present it in the world. He is the first of God's Messengers to reveal
the reality of a Greater Community of intelligent life in the universe.
The Messenger has been engaged in a process of Revelation for over
30 years. He is alive in the world today.

THE PRESENCE can refer to either the presence of Knowledge
within the individual, the Presence of the Angelic Assembly or

ultimately the Presence of God. The Presence of these three realities offers a life-changing experience of grace and relationship that can be found by following the mystery in life and by studying and practicing either one of God's past Revelations or God's New Revelation for the world. The New Revelation offers a modern pathway to experiencing the power of this Presence in your life.

STEPS TO KNOWLEDGE is an ancient book of spiritual practice now being given by God to the world for the first time. In taking this mysterious journey, each person is led to the discovery of the power of Knowledge and the experience of profound inner knowing, which can lead them to their higher purpose and calling in life.

THE GREATER COMMUNITY is the larger universe of intelligent life in which our world has always existed. This Greater Community encompasses all worlds in the universe where sentient life exists, in all states of evolution and development. The New Message reveals that humanity is in an early and adolescent phase of its development and that the time has now come for humanity to prepare to emerge into the Greater Community. It is here, standing at the threshold of space, that humanity discovers that it is not alone in the universe, or even within its own world.

THE GREATER COMMUNITY WAY OF KNOWLEDGE represents God's Work in the universe, which is to reclaim the separated in all worlds through the power of Knowledge that is inherent in all intelligent life. To understand what God is doing in our world, we must begin to understand what God is doing in the entire universe. For the first time in history, The Greater Community Way of Knowledge is being presented to the world through a New Message from God. The New Message opens the portal to this timeless Work of God underway throughout the Greater Community of life in the universe. We who stand at the threshold of emerging into this Greater

Community must have access to this greater reality and this pathway of redemption in order to understand our future and destiny as a race.

THE GREATER DARKNESS is an Intervention underway by certain races from the Greater Community who are here to take advantage of a weak and divided humanity. This Intervention is occurring at a time when the human family is entering a period of increasing breakdown and disorder, in the face of the Great Waves of change. The Intervention presents itself as a benign and redeeming force while in reality its ultimate goal is to undermine human freedom and self-determination and take control of the world and its resources. The New Message reveals that the Intervention seeks to secretly establish its influence here in the minds and hearts of people at a time of growing confusion, conflict and vulnerability. As the native peoples of this world, we are called upon to oppose this Intervention and to alert and educate others, thus uniting the human family in a great common purpose and preparing our world for the challenges and opportunities of life in the Greater Community.

THE GREAT WAVES OF CHANGE are a set of powerful environmental, economic and social forces now converging upon the world. The Great Waves are the result of humanity's misuse and overuse of the world, its resources and its environment. The Great Waves have the power to drastically alter the face of the world—producing economic instability, runaway climate change, violent weather and the loss of arable land and freshwater resources, threatening to produce a world condition of great difficulty and human suffering. The Great Waves are not an end times or apocalyptic event, but instead a period of transition to a new world condition. The New Message reveals what is coming for the world and the greater preparation that must be undertaken by enough people.

It is calling for human unity and cooperation born now out of sheer necessity for the preservation and protection of human civilization.

HIGHER PURPOSE refers to the specific contribution each person was sent into the world to make and the unique relationships that will enable the fulfillment of this purpose. Knowledge within the individual holds their higher purpose and destiny for them, which cannot be ascertained by the intellect alone. These must be discovered, followed and expressed in service to others to be fully realized. The world needs the demonstration of this higher purpose from many more people as never before.

SPIRITUAL FAMILY refers to the small working groups formed after the Separation to enable all individuals to work towards greater states of union and relationship, undertaking this over a long span of time, culminating in their final return to God. Your Spiritual Family represents the relationships you have reclaimed through Knowledge during your long journey through Separation. Some members of your Spiritual Family are in the world and some are beyond the world. The Spiritual Families are a part of the mysterious Plan of God to free and reunite all those living in Separation.

ANCIENT HOME refers to the reality of life and the state of awareness and relationship you had before entering the world, and to which you will return after your life in the world. Your Ancient Home is a state of connection and relationship with your Spiritual Family, The Assembly and God.

THE MESSENGER

Marshall Vian Summers is the Messenger for the New Message from God. For over three decades he has been the recipient of a vast New Revelation, given to prepare humanity for the great environmental, social and economic changes that are coming to the world and for humanity's emergence into a universe of intelligent life.

In 1982, at the age of 33, Marshall Vian Summers had a direct encounter with the Angelic Presence who had been guiding and preparing him for his future role and calling. This encounter forever altered the course of his life and initiated him into a deeper relationship with the Angelic Assembly, requiring that he surrender his life to God. This began the long, mysterious process of receiving God's New Message for humanity.

Following this mysterious initiation, he received the first revelations of the New Message from God. Over the decades since, a vast Revelation for humanity has unfolded, at times slowly and at times in great torrents. During these long years, he had to proceed with the support of only a few individuals, not knowing what this growing Revelation would mean and where it would ultimately lead.

The Messenger has walked a long and difficult road to receive and present the largest Revelation ever given to the human family. Still today the Voice of Revelation continues to flow through him as he faces the great challenge of bringing God's New Revelation to a troubled and conflicted world.

Read and hear the Story of the Messenger:
www.newmessage.org/story

Hear and watch the world teachings of the Messenger:
www.newmessage.org/messenger

The Voice of Revelation

For the first time in history, you can hear the Voice of Revelation, such a Voice as spoke to the prophets and Messengers of the past and is now speaking again through a new Messenger who is in the world today.

The Voice of Revelation is not the voice of one individual, but that of the entire Angelic Assembly speaking together, all as one. Here God communicates beyond words to the Angelic Assembly, who then translate God's Message into human words and language that we can comprehend.

The revelations of this book were originally spoken in this manner by the Voice of Revelation through the Messenger Marshall Vian Summers. This process of Divine Revelation has occurred since 1982. The Revelation continues to this day.

———— ❧ ————

The original audio recordings of the Voice of Revelation
are made available to all people.
To hear the Voice, which is the source of
the text contained in this book and throughout
the New Message, please visit:
www.newmessage.org/experience

To learn more about the Voice of Revelation, what it is
and how it speaks through the Messenger, visit:
www.newmessage.org/voiceofrevelation

About The Society for the New Message from God

Founded in 1992 by Marshall Vian Summers, The Society for the New Message from God is an independent religious 501(c)(3) non-profit organization that is primarily supported by readers and students of the New Message, receiving no sponsorship or revenue from any government or religious organization.

The Society's mission is to bring the New Message from God to people everywhere so that humanity can find its common ground, preserve the Earth, protect human freedom and advance human civilization as we stand at the threshold of emerging into a Greater Community of intelligent life in the universe.

Marshall Vian Summers and The Society have been given the immense responsibility of bringing the New Message into the world. The members of The Society are a small group of dedicated individuals who have committed their lives to fulfill this mission. For them, it is a burden and a great blessing to give themselves wholeheartedly in this great service to humanity.

The Society for the New Message

Contact us:

P.O. Box 1724 Boulder, CO 80306-1724
(303) 938-8401 (800) 938-3891
011 303 938 84 01 (International)
(303) 938-1214 (fax)
society@newmessage.org
www.newmessage.org
www.alliesofhumanity.org
www.newknowledgelibrary.org

Connect with us:

www.youtube.com/thenewmessagefromgod
www.facebook.com/newmessagefromgod
www.facebook.com/marshallsummers
www.twitter.com/godsnewmessage

ABOUT THE WORLDWIDE COMMUNITY OF THE NEW MESSAGE FROM GOD

The New Message from God is being shared by people around the world. Representing more than 90 countries and over 23 languages, a worldwide community of students has formed to receive and study the New Message and to support the mission of the Messenger and The Society.

Learn more about the worldwide community of people who are learning and living the New Message from God and taking the Steps to Knowledge towards a new and inspired life.

Become a part of a worldwide community of people who are pioneering a new chapter in the human experience. The New Message has the power to awaken the sleeping brilliance in people everywhere and bring new inspiration and wisdom into the lives of people from all nations and faith traditions.

———————

Hear the Voice of Revelation speaking directly
on the purpose and importance of the Worldwide Community:
www.newmessage.org/theworldwidecommunity

Learn more about the educational opportunities available in the
Worldwide Community:

Forum - www.newmessage.org/forum
Free School - www.newmessage.org/school
Live Internet Broadcasts and International Events -
www.newmessage.org/events
Annual Encampment - www.newmessage.org/encampment
Online Library and Study Pathway - www.newmessage.org/experience

Books of the New Message from God

God Has Spoken Again

The One God

The New Messenger

Greater Community Spirituality

Relationships & Higher Purpose

Living The Way of Knowledge

Steps to Knowledge

Life in the Universe

The Great Waves of Change

Wisdom from the Greater Community I & II

Secrets of Heaven